THE JUMBO BOOK OF ART

Kids Can Press acknowledges the financial support of the Ontario Arts Council, the Canada Council for the Arts and the Government of Canada, through the BPIDP, for our publishing activity.

Published in Canada by
Kids Can Press Ltd.
29 Birch Avenue
Toronto, ON M4V 1E2

Published in the U.S. by
Kids Can Press Ltd.
2250 Military Road
Tonawanda, NY 14150

www.kidscanpress.com

Edited by Linda Biesenthal and Stacey Roderick
Designed by Karen Powers
Printed in Hong Kong, China

This book is limp sewn with a drawn-on cover.

CM PA 03 0 9 8 7 6 5 4 3 2 1

National Library of Canada Cataloguing in Publication Data

Luxbacher, Irene, 1970–
    The jumbo book of art / written and illustrated by Irene Luxbacher.
On cover: An artistic adventure from the Avenue Road Arts School
Includes index.
ISBN 1-55074-762-2

1. Art — Technique — Juvenile literature. I. Title.
N7440.L89 2003   j701'.8   C2002-905569-5

Kids Can Press is a *forus*™ Entertainment company

Dedication

To the artists at the Avenue Road Arts School for inspiring this book, and to my parents, Frank and Sophia, and my brother, Nick, whose love and encouragement kept me going throughout this adventure.

Acknowledgments

This book evolved over a period of nearly five years, during which many people contributed. The project ideas originated with the amazing and talented artists and instructors at the Avenue Road Arts School, most particularly Liana Del Mastro Vicente, Julie Frost, Leslie Graham, Martha Johnson, Joni Moriyama, Eric Neighbour, Linda Prussick, Cynthia Sneath, Susie Whaley and Russell Zeid. Also, this book would not have been possible without the patience, talents and expertise of everyone at Kids Can Press, particularly Valerie Hussey, Rivka Cranley, Linda Biesenthal, Stacey Roderick, Karen Powers and Mike Reis. And a very special thank you to Lola Rasminsky, Director of the Avenue Road Arts School. Her remarkable vision, effort and support of arts education continue to make a difference.

I would also like to thank Joni Moriyama for the use of her clay ram's head on page 107, Julie Frost for the use of her mythical scroll on page 175 and Susie Whaley for the use of her treasure box on the bottom of page 181. And thanks to Colin and Meredith Gibson for being my photo inspirations for the Awesome Originals (page 44) and Face Map (page 46 and cover) projects.

A portion of the proceeds from the sale of this book will be used to support the activities of Arts for Children of Toronto, a registered charity associated with the Avenue Road Arts School. Through scholarship and outreach programs, Arts for Children of Toronto provides high quality arts experiences to thousands of children who might not otherwise enjoy these opportunities.

An artistic adventure from the
Avenue Road Arts School

KIDS · CAN · PRESS

The JUMBO

BOOK OF

ART

Written and illustrated by
Irene Luxbacher

KIDS CAN PRESS

e N T S

Welcome to the Avenue Road Arts School's book of amazing artistic adventure! At the Avenue Road Arts School, we believe art is more than sketched out images, painted pictures or awesome 3-D objects. Art is an adventure — an exciting opportunity to draw out your best ideas, to mix information with imagination, to create with confidence and to inspire others. It's a road to discovery — and you're bound to find lots of artistic brilliance buried inside you.

ON THE ROAD TO ARTISTIC ADVENTURE

Each small step you take — whether it's drawing a simple cartoon, painting a postcard of paradise, sculpting a dreadful dragon or creating a treasure box — will give you a feeling of artistic accomplishment. And, along the road, you'll find out how good it feels to follow in the footsteps of artists through the ages. We hope that these artistic adventures will fill you up with lots of ideas to keep you traveling for a long time to come.

Here are a few Avenue Road ideas to take along on your artistic adventure.

● Travel light

Leave nasty doubts and heavy expectations behind. There's nothing worse than being bogged down with baggage when you're traveling through new terrain.

Don't need this or this or this.

● Make mistakes

Lots of them. It's a good way of making sure that your artistic adventures never get dull. Mistakes can turn into unexpected avenues for exploration if you learn to look at them as "happy accidents."

Hey, that's neat.

● Have fun

This is the most important rule. If you are not having fun or feel frustrated, don't give up — just take a short breather or a long break.

I think I need a break.

● Be your own boss

The only person you have to listen to when it comes to deciding which direction to take — or deciding which project to start with — is you.

I think I'll start here.

● Stay safe

Make sure you read the labels of your materials for any warnings and instructions. If you have an allergy to any of the materials we suggest (for example, some people are allergic to latex), ask your local art or craft store to recommend an alternative. Also, be very careful using adult tools, such as knives or glue guns. When in doubt, get help from an older artistic adventurer.

So pack your bags and head for the hills — or turn the page. The road to artistic adventure awaits. From all of us at the Avenue Road Arts School, bon voyage, have lots of fun — and we'll see you on the road!

DRAWING
out your ideas

Walk this way and get ready to draw out some of these ideas!

Quirky Creatures
(page 14)

The Big Picture
(page 12)

On the Move
(page 17)

Land of Illusion
(page 18)

Highlight Event

In the Shadows

Face Map

Magic Mirror

Yellow Brick Road

In the Dark

Comic Creation

In the Drawing Studio

Here are some tools and materials you can use to draw out your most creative ideas.

charcoal

pastels

pencils

sketchbooks

colored markers

colored pencils

erasers

crayons

ink

ink pen
and brushes

ruler

black markers

X-Acto knife

scissors

paint and
paintbrushes

construction paper

THE BIG PICTURE

Stand back and draw from a distance. When you look at the big picture, you'll see a lovely landscape hiding in a few simple lines and silly scribbles.

Artist's Tools

- big sheet of paper
- masking tape
- long stick
- colored chalk or artist's charcoal
- fine-tip marker

1 Tape the big sheet of paper to a wall or the floor.

2 Tape the chalk or charcoal to the long stick.

3 Take a big step back.

- Draw some very vertical lines.

- Create some crazy shapes.

- Add some silly scribbles.

- Dab on a dozen dots.

4 Have a good look to see what's hiding in your landscape. Then grab your marker and step up to the big picture.

- Draw some leafy treetops.
- Fill in a few special features.
- Make flying birds.
- Add some finishing touches.

5 Stand back and enjoy the view.

Charcoal Sketches

In the 1500s, artists in Europe began using specially made charcoal attached to a cane to sketch large-scale drawings for frescoes and murals. Charcoal is a great tool for sketching because it's very easy to erase.

QUIRKY CREATURES

You'll find lots of quirky creatures hiding in a page filled with different lines and shapes. All you have to do is draw them out.

There's also an artist's secret lurking here. Did you know that a line is just a path between two dots? And that a shape starts and ends at the same dot?

Artist's Tools

- paper
- water-soluble pencil or chalk

3 Pick some dots and make some basic shapes — circles, squares, triangles and rectangles — and some curvy ones.

4 To spot some quirky creatures, try turning your paper upside down or sideways.

1 Fill your page with lots of dots.

2 Connect pairs of dots to make different kinds of lines that run in different directions.

5 Outline the creatures you've spotted.

6 With a wet finger or tissue, erase the dots, lines and shapes that don't belong to your quirky creatures.

7 Add some smudges, smears and details to draw out the character of your creatures.

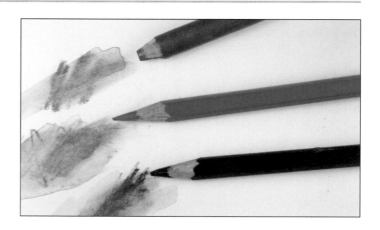

Water-Soluble Pencils

Water-soluble pencils are great for making marks you can smudge and smear with a wet finger or tissue.

Line Up!

You can change the character of your quirky creatures by
using different types of lines and different drawing tools.
Try some of these.

fat lines    **thin lines**

loud lines    **soft lines**

sad lines    **mad lines**

worry lines    **laugh lines**

On the Move!

Use a few lines and shapes to add
a little life to your quirky creatures.

walking lines

jumping lines

running lines

flying lines

LAND OF ILLUSION

Like magicians, artists are great at creating illusions. Using a few simple artistic tricks, artists create the illusion of space and distance on a flat piece of paper. Avoid confusion in your land of illusion by keeping your eye on the horizon.

Artist's Tools

- large sheet of paper
- two colors of paint
- paintbrush
- old magazines
- scissors
- glue
- marker or pencil

1 Fold the paper in half and then open it up so the fold runs horizontally. This is your horizon line.

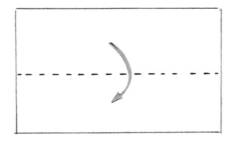

2 Start at the top of the paper and brush on the sky, all the way down to the horizon line.

3 Start at the bottom of the paper and brush on the earth, all the way up to the horizon line. Set aside to dry.

4 From old magazines, cut out some different-sized pictures of cars, houses, people, pets and other things you like. Cut carefully and close to the edge of your pictures.

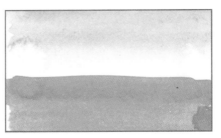

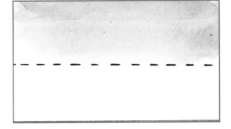

5 When your paint is dry, arrange and glue your cut-outs so that

- the smaller ones are near the horizon line
- the larger ones are near the edges of your page and farthest away from the horizon line
- the middle-sized ones are somewhere in between
- some are overlapping

6 With your marker or pencil, add some landscape features. Remember: the farther away things are, the fewer details you can see.

7 Add some different-sized quirky creatures and watch them pop right off your page!

Foreshortening

Foreshortening is the technique artists use to make things appear close up or farther away on a flat piece of paper.

YELLOW BRICK ROAD

Add a vanishing point on the horizon of your landscapes so you won't get lost in the distance. It's a trick artists use to create a landscape that looks as if you could step right inside and follow the yellow brick road to the end of the line!

Artist's Tools

- yellow crayon
- square piece of bristol board
- black or blue tempera paint
- squirt of dishwashing liquid
- paintbrush
- fat toothpick or safety pin

1 With your yellow crayon, completely color in the bristol board.

2 Add a squirt of dishwashing liquid to your paint to make it stick, and paint over your crayon-covered bristol board. Let dry.

3 Using your toothpick or safety pin, draw a horizon line at about the middle of your picture.

4 Mark a dot anywhere along the horizon line. This is your picture's vanishing point.

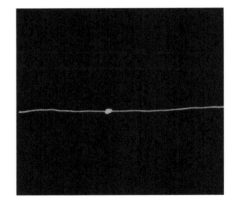

5 To construct your Yellow Brick Road, mark two dots at the bottom of your board, each one about 2.5 cm (1 in.) in from the side. Make a line from each dot to your vanishing point using your toothpick or pin. This is the end of the road — where all things seem to disappear.

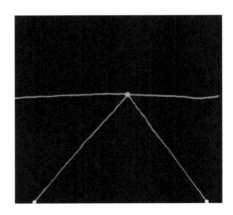

6 With your toothpick or safety pin, scratch in some details — bricks, trees, quirky creatures. Remember the rules of foreshortening: the closer things are to the horizon line, the smaller they appear, and the farther away things are from the horizon, the bigger they appear.

A Whole New Dimension

In the 1400s, artists started transforming a flat piece of paper, which has two dimensions (height and width), into an image that appears to have three dimensions (height, width and depth). They invented the technique of linear perspective, where parallel lines seem to meet at a vanishing point on the horizon line.

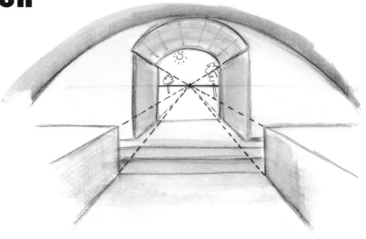

UNDER COVER

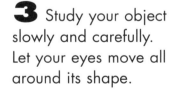

Sketching the shape of an object first makes it a lot easier to draw almost anything. By putting an object under cover, you can simplify its shape — and avoid getting all tied up in the details.

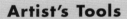
Artist's Tools

- an object you want to draw
- lots of string
- an old sheet or a piece of plain fabric
- drawing paper
- pencil

1 Cover up your object with the sheet or piece of fabric.

2 Tie the string as snugly as possible around the object so that all you can see is its shape.

3 Study your object slowly and carefully. Let your eyes move all around its shape.

4 Keep your eyes moving around the object and start sketching. Let your pencil follow your eyes.

5 When you're happy with your sketch, remove the cover.

6 Draw in some details.

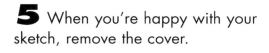
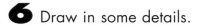

Blind Alley

Draw an object without lifting your pencil
and without looking at your page!
This is called a blind contour drawing.
It helps artists practice looking more
carefully at edges, outlines and shapes.

1 Pick a favorite object that has an
interesting shape and lots of detail.
Try your shoe, a bicycle, a pile
of books or a vase of flowers.

2 Study your object and start
drawing very slowly. Let your pencil
follow your eye around the contour
of your object. No peeking at your
page and no lifting your pencil off the
page. Your drawing should be one
continuous line.

Here are some blind contour
drawings. Can you guess
what they are?

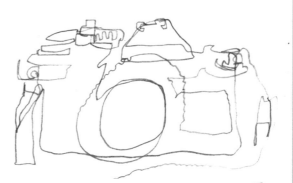

SKETCHBOOK STUDY #4

Helping Hand

Make a contour drawing of your hand — and then fill in all the details. This time you can watch what you're doing!

1 Draw the contour of your hand without taking your pencil off the page.

2 Draw in every bump, knuckle, hair, wrinkle and fingernail.

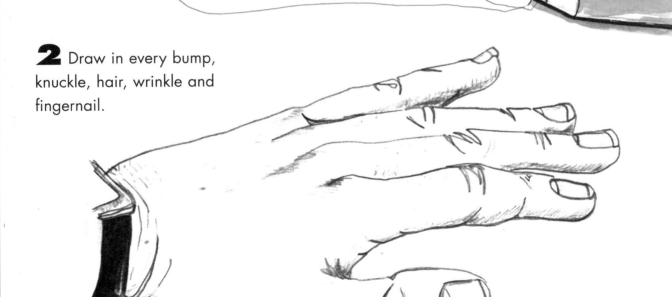

IN THE DARK

Dazzle your family and friends by drawing simple silhouettes in the dark. All it takes is some artistic tracing of shadowy outlines.

Artist's Tools

- darkened room
- large sheet of white paper
- masking tape
- table
- lamp or flashlight
- models and favorite objects
- pencil
- scissors
- black and white construction paper
- glue

1 In a darkened room, tape the large sheet of white paper to a wall.

2 Set the lamp (without its shade) or the flashlight on a table about a meter (3 ft.) in front of the paper. Shine the light on the paper.

3 Pose your model or object standing or sitting between the light and the paper. Move your light source back if you want a smaller silhouette.

4 With the pencil, trace around the shadowy silhouette you see on the paper. Cut out your silhouette.

5 Place the silhouette on the black construction paper and trace its outline.

6 Carefully cut out the black silhouette and glue it onto white construction paper.

Dazzling Drawings

Silhouette artists sometimes turn their black-on-white silhouettes into dazzling drawings by filling in some details with pens, paint or chalk. Try using a silver or gold pen to add details to your silhouettes.

Or make a silhouette scene by gluing a series of simple silhouettes of your favorite people and objects on white bristol board.

IN THE SHADOWS

What's that lurking in the shadows? It's another simple trick artists use to change flat shapes into forms that look 3-D. You can make your drawings come to life just by adding some shadows and shading.

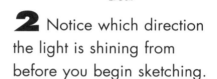

Artist's Tools

- a sunny day
- some ordinary or favorite objects
- paper
- pencil, pen and artist's charcoal

1 On a sunny day, arrange your objects outside in a place where the sun casts shadows on them. If there's no sun in sight, stay indoors and shine a lamp or flashlight on the objects.

2 Notice which direction the light is shining from before you begin sketching.

3 Using a soft pencil, lightly outline the shapes of the objects.

4 Go over the outlines with your pencil or an ink pen. Press harder on the side farthest away from the light source and very lightly on the side of the shapes closest to the light source.

5 Try these shadowy techniques.

• Smudge some charcoal.

• Scribble and scratch some lines.

• Use the side of your pencil.

• Dab and dot with the point of a pen.

HIGHLIGHT EVENT

Look on the bright side of things! Here are some valuable tips on how to turn a dark drawing into a real highlight event.

Artist's Tools

- a simple object
- small table
- lamp or flashlight
- black construction paper
- white pencil, chalk or crayon

1 Place the object on a small table and shine a lamp or flashlight on it.

2 First, check out the direction of your light source and study your object, looking for this light logic.

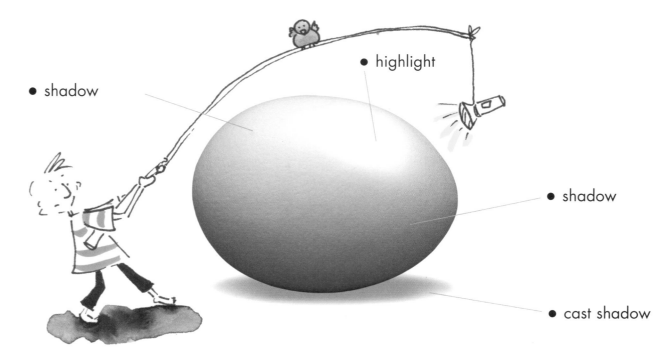

- shadow
- highlight
- shadow
- cast shadow

3 Use a white colored pencil to lightly sketch in the shape you see.

4 Press harder on the side of the object that is closer to the light and more lightly on the side that is farther away.

5 Use the side of your colored pencil to blend or smudge.

6 Use the point of your colored pencil to stipple or cross-hatch.

Chiaroscuro

Chiaroscuro means the balance of light and shadow in a picture. Try erasing highlights into dark pencil or charcoal drawings.

Gray Scale

Draw a few simple objects. Practice adding shadows and shading by smudging, stippling and cross-hatching using different tools — soft pencil, ink pen and charcoal.

smudging

cross-hatching

stippling

Try making gradual changes from very light shadows to very dark shadows.

cross-hatching

stippling

smudging

Use different shading techniques and materials to create a gray scale.

From 2-D to 3-D

Pull out all your artistic tricks and practice turning

- a circle into a sphere

- a square into a cube

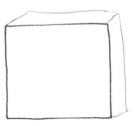 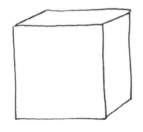 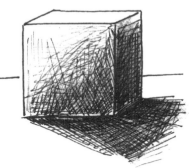

- a triangle into a pyramid

  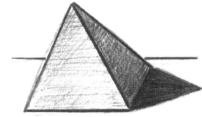

TOUCHY TEXTURES

What does the bark of a tree or a sidewalk or a wooden fence feel like when you touch it? Make your drawings look touchable by adding some texture.

Artist's Tools

- a walk in the park or a tour of your room
- sheets of drawing paper
- charcoal, pencil or crayon
- scissors
- glue
- piece of bristol board

1 Take a walk in the park and find some objects with different textures — leaves, tree bark, the seat of a swing, the steps of a slide.

If it's raining, take a tour of your room to turn up some different textures — a window screen, the floor, Lego blocks, coins, your blue jeans.

2 Put a sheet of paper over each object. Using charcoal, a pencil or a crayon, rub over the surface so that the texture appears on your paper.

3 Cut out a different shape from each of your rubbings.

4 Arrange the shapes on the bristol board. When you like what you see, glue them into place.

5 Now draw your collage! On a sheet of drawing paper, first sketch the shapes and then try to copy the different textures.

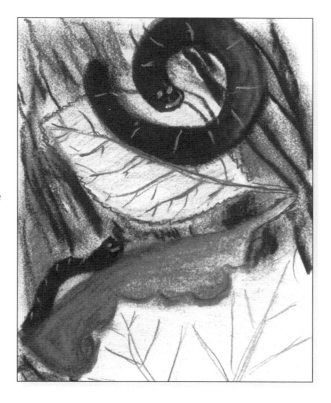

Touchy Tips

Here are some drawing tips.

• Use solid, fat marker lines for hard, smooth surfaces.

• Use soft charcoal smudges for a warm and fuzzy touch.

• Use squirrelly pencil scribbles for hilarious hairy textures.

• Use scratchy lines for picky prickles.

SIMPLE STILL LIFE

"Check" this out! Create a simple still-life composition on a checkerboard tablecloth using your favorite objects. Choose a variety of objects with different shapes, sizes, colors and textures.

Artist's Tools

- collection of favorite objects
- pastel-colored paper or drawing paper
- pencil
- ruler
- eraser
- colored pencils or chalk

1 Draw a horizon line on your sheet of paper.

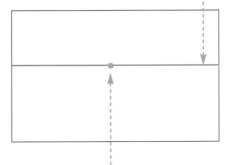

Add a vanishing point on the horizon line.

2 Using a pencil and ruler, mark every centimeter (half-inch) along the bottom and sides of your paper up to the horizon line.

3 With a pencil and a ruler, draw a light line from the vanishing point to each mark.

4 Draw a horizontal line about 2.5 cm (1 in.) from the bottom of your page.

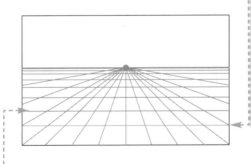

Draw another horizontal line about 2 cm (¾ in.) above the first one. Making the space between the horizontal lines smaller each time, repeat this step until there's no space left.

5 Arrange your objects on a table. Sketch them on your checkered drawing. Use the checkered pattern as a guideline.

- Objects on top of small checks are at the back of your composition.

- Objects on top of big checks are at the front.

- Objects near the front cover or overlap objects behind them.

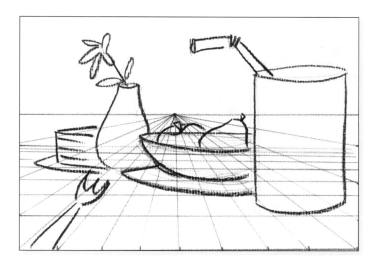

6 Erase overlapping lines and shapes.

7 Fill in the checks with brown or black and white colored pencils or chalk, alternating so that you make a checkerboard pattern.

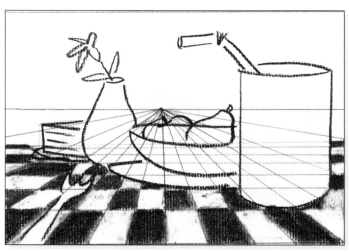

8 Use brown or black and white colored pencils or chalk to add shadows, highlights and textures.

9 Color in your still life.

INVENT AND SKETCH

Invent a crazy still life and then sketch it. When you're finished, take your still life apart and see if a friend can put it back together again by looking at your sketch.

Artist's Tools

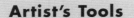

- stool or table
- crazy covering
- collection of fun objects of different shapes, sizes and textures
- large pad of drawing paper or newsprint
- pencil or charcoal
- eraser, if needed
- easel and drawing board, bulldog clip

Invent

1 On a stool or a small table, spread out your crazy covering.

2 With your collection of fun objects, create a composition full of interesting shapes, forms and spaces.

3 Clip your paper to a drawing board and place it on your easel, or lay it flat on a nearby table.

Sketch

4 Use your pencil, graphite stick or charcoal.

• Draw some simple shapes.

• Outline interesting spaces.

• Fill in forms with shadows.

• Add highlights.

• Create textures.

Creative Compositions

Artists use these compositional shapes to help them organize the objects or elements of their pictures. They keep moving objects around until they like what they see.

Totally Spacey

Practice looking at how an object and the space around it fit together like pieces of a puzzle. Artists call the space that the object takes up positive space and the space around it negative space.

1 Set an object with a simple shape — a bottle or a vase or a block — on a table and sketch its outline.

2 Use two different colors of chalk, pencil or marker to create positive and negative space.

SKETCHBOOK STUDY #8

It's All Relative

Use a pencil as a measuring tool and make a drawing of your bed. Start by closing one eye and stretching out your arm with pencil in hand.

1 How tall is your bed "relative" or compared to the size of your pencil?

2 How wide is your bed relative to its length?

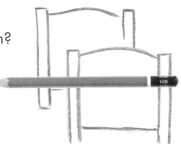

3 Use your pencil to figure out angles.

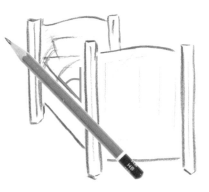

By making comparisons or looking for relationships, artists can "see" how to draw almost anything.

MAGIC MIRROR

"Magic Mirror, help me see the person staring back at me!" Here's a self-portrait that reflects who you really are — or who you want to be.

Artist's Tools

- mirror or piece of Mylar (available at art shops)
- cardboard
- glue
- scissors
- markers or crayon
- wooden dowel, garden stick or cardboard tube
- duct tape
- beads, paints, Plasticine, feathers, glitter, fun finds, pipe cleaners, etc.

Frame Yourself

On the cardboard, draw a frame shape that shows your true self. A big square? A bit of zigzag? A huge hat? Cut out the frame and glue on the mirror or Mylar.

Reflect Yourself

Use markers to draw your inner self around the edges of your frame.

princely patterns   crazy curls   mysterious marks

Get a Handle on Yourself

Attach a wooden dowel, garden stick or cardboard tube to the back of your mirror with duct tape.

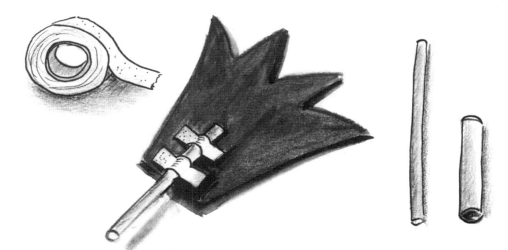

Draw Yourself

Look into the mirror. With a marker or crayon, draw what you see right on your reflection.

Decorate Yourself

Decorate the mirror frame with paints, Plasticine, paper cut-outs, beads, buttons, glitter, etc.

AWESOME ORIGINALS

Turn your school picture into awesome originals and fantasy faces. Share them with the world by adding frames and hanging them on your own Wall of Fame.

Artist's Tools

- school picture
- pencil, ink pen, markers, colored pencils
- drawing paper, tracing paper, construction paper, patterned paper, acetate
- bristol board
- scissors
- glue

1 Create different kinds of copies of your school picture.

- Trace a copy using a marker on tracing paper or acetate (clear plastic found in art supply stores).

- Make a photocopy on a photocopier.

- Sketch a copy using your favorite drawing tool and paper.

2 Add different funny features and special effects to each of your portraits.

- Draw in some details.

- Glue on a colorful collage of patterned paper scraps.

- Add some bold shapes and spaces with markers.

Frame It!

Use a piece of bristol board or cardboard that's slightly larger than your portraits. Decorate the frame to suit yourself!

FACE MAP

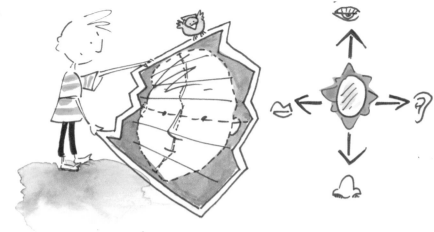

When artists draw a portrait, they start with a sketch that looks a bit like a map. This helps them get the eyes in the right place, the ears the right size and the nose where a nose goes.

Artist's Tools

- photo of yourself
- drawing paper
- pencil

1 First, study your photo face. Use your pencil to measure the size of your eyes, nose, mouth, ears and the distances between them.

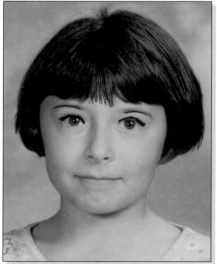

2 Sketch the shape of your head.

Oval, rectangular and heart-shaped are basic head shapes.

3 Sketch in two lines that divide your head shape into four equal parts.

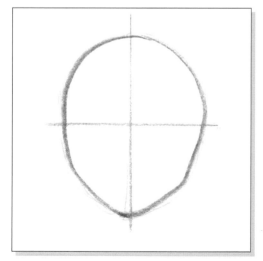

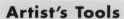

4 Here's how to find your features.

- Your eyes are in the center of your head.

- Your ears start around eye level and end at the bottom of your nose.

- Your nose grows in the middle of your face.

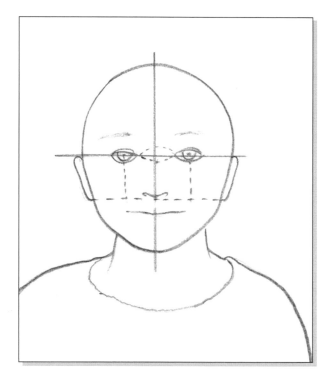

- The distance between your eyes is about the length of one eye.

- Your mouth runs from the middle of one eye to the middle of the other.

5 Study your photo face again, looking carefully at the outline and shape of each of your features. Or look in a mirror. Are your eyes sad? Do your nostrils flare? Play with your sketch until you see yourself staring back.

6 Add hair and some soft shadows and highlights.

BODY PARTS

Drawing people may not be as hard as you think! Make your drawings of people fall into place by piecing your own body parts together.

Artist's Tools

- pencil
- large sheets of paper or bristol board
- scissors
- hole punch and string or brass fasteners
- masking tape

1 On a large sheet of paper, carefully trace each of these body parts. If tracing yourself is too hard, ask a friend to help.

- upper torso
- lower torso
- thighs
- neck
- head

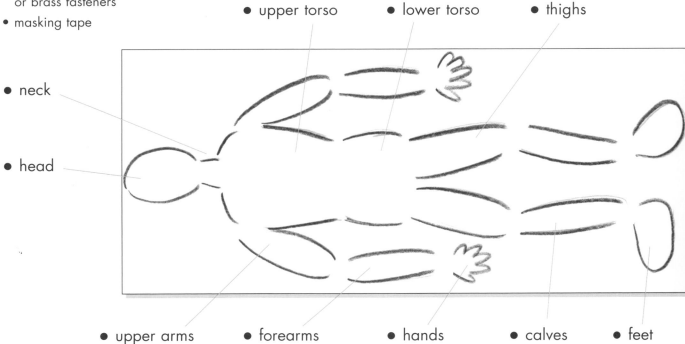

- upper arms
- forearms
- hands
- calves
- feet

2 Cut out all your body parts.

3 Piece yourself together! With a hole punch and string or brass fasteners, attach your body parts at the joints.

- elbows
- wrists

- neck
- shoulder
- waist
- hips
- knees
- ankles

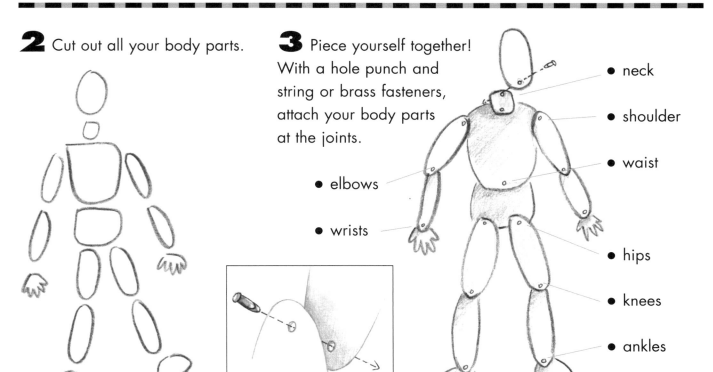

4 Tape your body to a wall using masking tape.

5 Experiment with lots of poses and positions by moving around your jointed body parts.

Measure Up!

Did you know that the average adult stands between seven and eight heads high? And that your hips are right in the middle of your body? Get out a measuring stick and a mirror and check out your body-part proportions.

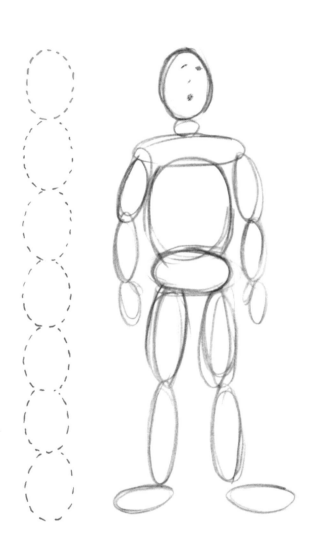

- How many heads tall are you?

- How long are your arms in relation to your body?

- Do your hands reach halfway to your knees when you're standing?

- Are your legs the same length as the rest of your body?

- How long are your thighs relative to your whole leg?

- Are your feet twice as long as your hands?

Using these calculations, make a rough sketch of your body. No details — just use a series of ovals for all your body parts.

Lively Life Drawings

Find a full-length mirror and strike some poses.
Practice drawing yourself

● bending over

● sitting down

● sneaking away

● jumping for joy

SO SURREAL!

Every artistic adventure is filled with some strange twists and turns. Create a work of art inspired by your wild imagination, a weird dream or accidental arrangement.

Artist's Tools

- one of your still life, landscape or figure drawings
- old magazines, calendars or ads
- scissors or X-Acto knife
- glue
- bristol board
- fine-tip ink pen, markers or colored pencils

1 Choose a still life, landscape or figure drawing or painting you've already made, or create a new one on a piece of bristol board.

2 Carefully cut out a few images and words from your favorite ads, posters, calendars or magazines. Be sure to cut close to the edges of your images. If you use an X-Acto knife, ask an adult to help.

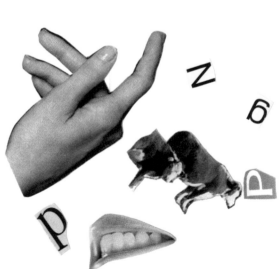

3 Set the cut-outs on top of your drawing and move them around until you've got a wild or weird arrangement.

For a really strange arrangement, stand on a chair and drop the cut-outs on your drawing. Glue the cut-outs into place.

4 Glue more words or images on your drawing in the strangest spots, such as a tadpole on top of a tutu. The stranger the better.

5 Use a fine-tip drawing pen, markers or colored pencils to add a few fun details to your drawings.

- Play with size and scale.

- Put in some speech bubbles.

COMIC CREATION

Time to draw out your own artistic adventure and turn it into a comic creation.

Artist's Tools

- sketchbook
- large sheet of paper
- pencil and ruler
- fine-tip ink pen
- markers, poster paints or colored pencils

1 Have some fun racking your brains for a good story idea. Here are the things a good story needs:

- a setting
- villains and heroes
- a problem that the villains create and the heroes fix
- lots of action

2 Where does your story take place?

- In a medieval castle?
- On another planet?
- Aboard a ship on the high seas?

3 In your sketchbook, create some comic characters.

• Cool superheroes?

• Amazing animals?

• Villainous Vikings?

4 Lay out your story.

• On a large sheet of paper, draw six panels, one for each scene.

• Organize your scenes into a simple story line using quick sketches.

Evil Viking ship approaches mythical land in far-off galaxy.

Evil Viking tries to destroy mythical land with lasers.

Hero enters picture as evil Viking continues the attack.

Hero deflects evil Viking's lasers with shield.

Lasers are deflected onto nearby planet – the home of a ferocious dragon.

Awakened dragon chases away evil Viking. Mythical land is saved.

5 Start another copy of your comic creation, this time adding the detail and drama with:

- foreshortened figures
- interesting shapes and spaces
- speech bubbles
- facial expressions

6 Trace or re-draw your sketched-out comic creation on a new sheet of paper with an ink pen, colored pencils, markers and/or poster paints. Add the story or text to your speech bubbles.

Creating with Color

Open the door and step into the
wonderful world of watercolors,
sunny acrylic skies and pastel portraits.

Postcards from Paradise (page 74)

Bright Summer Bouquet
(page 78)

Winter Wonderland
(page 80)

All Wrapped Up
(page 86)

Striking Stained Glass
(page 62)

Flying Fish
(page 92)

Make a Wish!
(page 90)

Great Graffiti
(page 66)

**Swashbuckling
Seascape**
(page 84)

Starry Sky
(page 94)

Crazy Carpet
(page 70)

In the Painting Studio

There are tons of tools and materials you can use to express your most colorful ideas.

paint palette

acrylic paints

paint roller

latex paints

wide brushes

palette knife

paintbrushes

watercolor paints

chalk pastels

watercolor palette

acrylic varnish

sponges

tempera paints

plastic containers

STRIKING STAINED GLASS

Create a unique stained-glass window. Use your favorite colors and shapes to tell a simple story, communicate a message or make a dandy design. Then, let the sun shine in!

Artist's Tools

- bright window
- scissors
- clear cellophane or plastic wrap
- masking tape
- newspapers
- thin black tape
- colored and metallic markers
- dishwashing liquid
- plastic containers
- liquid tempera paints
- different-sized brushes
- colored tissue paper or cellophane

1 Cut a sheet of clear cellophane or plastic wrap to fit on a bright window. Smooth out the sheet on the window. Tape the corners if necessary. Cover the windowsill and floor with newspapers.

2 Using the black tape, divide your sheet into geometric-shaped sections — triangles, squares, rectangles or circles.

3 With your colored markers, draw your story, message or design in the sections.

4 Add a few drops of dishwashing liquid to some plastic containers, and pour in your favorite paint colors. (The soap helps paint stick to a slippery surface.)

5 Color in your picture or design. Use fat brushes to fill in big spaces and small brushes for delicate details. Metallic markers look especially spectacular!

6 Cut out a few fun designs from small pieces of colored tissue paper or cellophane and gently press them into any freshly painted (wet) parts that seem a little plain. This will create a lovely layered look.

Remarkable Rainbow

Red, yellow and blue are called primary colors. You mix two primary colors together to make secondary colors — orange, violet and green. Use paints to practice turning these color combinations into a remarkable rainbow.

Red + **Blue** = **Violet**

Blue + **Yellow** = **Green**

Yellow + **Red** = **Orange**

Try the same thing with chalk pastels. When using chalk pastels, press each color firmly on the piece of paper. Use your finger or an eraser to smudge or blend them into one another.

Color Wheel Mandala

Some artists use color wheels to help them mix their colors.
Here's how to make your own.

1 Cut a large circle out of bristol board. Divide the circle into six equal pieces of pie.

2 Paint in the primary colors (red, blue, yellow) as shown. Then mix your paints to fill in secondary colors (orange, violet, green).

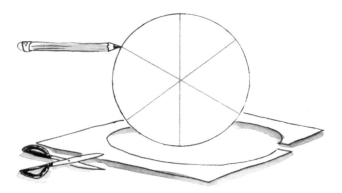

3 Transform your color wheel into a magnificent mandala — a spiritual symbol that's usually a circle with a square in the middle. Cut out a square or rectangle from another piece of bristol board and glue it to the center of your wheel. Decorate the square with painted, drawn and/or collaged designs and images that mean something special to you.

GREAT GRAFFITI

Let your favorite music inspire some great graffiti! This is an action painting to have fun with.

Artist's Tools

- old clothes
- large wall, indoors or out
- masking tape
- large piece of craft paper
- newspapers
- acrylic or tempera paints
- containers for paints
- paintbrushes, big and small
- paint rollers
- plastic knife or palette knife
- spray bottles filled with water or diluted paints
- buckets of water for cleaning brushes and rollers
- favorite piece of music

1 Put on some old clothes.

2 Spread some newspapers on the ground, and tape more to the wall. Tape the large piece of craft paper to the wall.

3 Mix the paints in containers that are large enough for your brushes and rollers. If you're using a plastic or palette knife, be sure you have some thick paint to work with.

4 Put on your favorite piece of music and let loose! Cover your entire surface with spontaneous marks and movements.

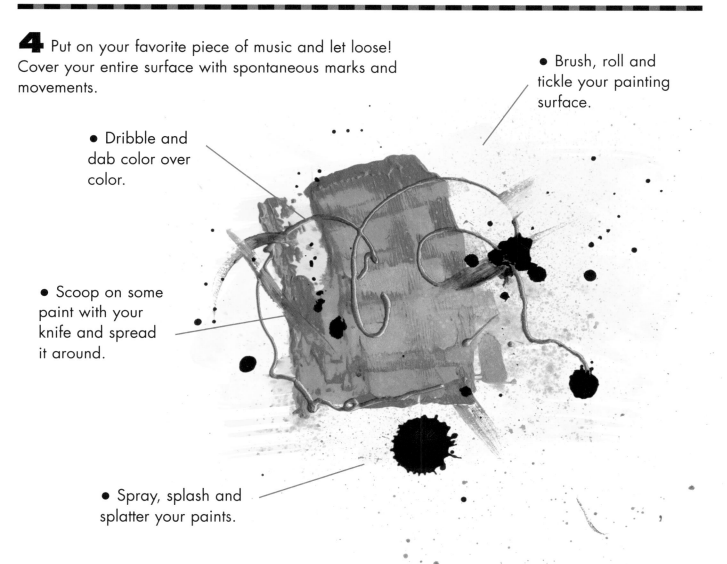

• Brush, roll and tickle your painting surface.

• Dribble and dab color over color.

• Scoop on some paint with your knife and spread it around.

• Spray, splash and splatter your paints.

Colorful Chords

Just as the notes played on a musical instrument can create harmonies you hear, colors can create harmonies you see.

Can you find any color combinations or chords that seem large and loud? What about soft and sweet?

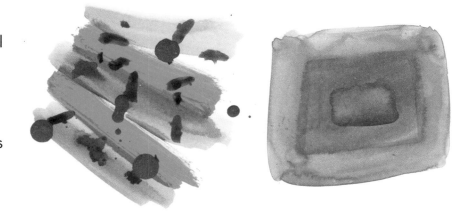

Primed for Painting

Try painting on wood, cardboard, papier-mâché sculptures or canvas. Canvas is a special cloth that lots of artists paint on and is available at art supply shops.

Whatever surface you choose, you'll have to prime, or prepare, it first. Make sure your surface is clean, and then brush on two coats of latex or acrylic paint. Let dry.

The color of paint that you use to prime your surface will affect the colors you paint on top.

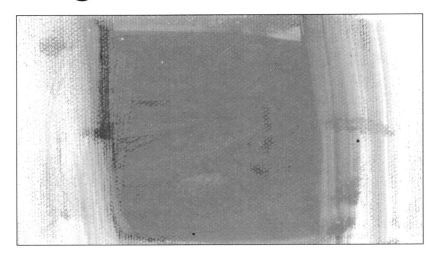

A surface primed with white can make colors seem bright and cheerful.

A surface primed with black or brown can make colors seem dark and heavy.

A Perfect Palette

Besides the surface you mix paint on, "palette" also means the range of colors that an artist uses. Expand your palette!

Try mixing a color paint with

- **white** to make **tints**.
Use tints for highlights
or to soften colors.

- **black** to make **shades**.
Use shades to make shadows
or to darken colors.

- **black and white or gray** to make **tones**.
Use tones to make colors faded or dull.

CRAZY CARPET

A jungle mat? A cosmic carpet? A rosy rug? What kind of crazy carpet would you like to live with?

Artist's Tools

- newspapers
- carpet-sized piece of heavy canvas
- latex primer
- pencil or charcoal
- acrylic paints
- containers or palette for mixing paints
- paintbrushes, sponges, palette knife, other painting tools
- acrylic varnish, flat or matte
- safety goggles and mask

1 Spread newspapers on the floor and stretch your canvas out on top.

2 Prime the canvas by brushing on two coats of white latex paint or primer. Let dry.

3 Think of a theme or a scene for your carpet. Sketch your ideas on the canvas with a pencil or charcoal.

4 Mix your paint colors. Your paints can be thick and gloppy, silky smooth or really runny. Add water to get the consistency that's right for your carpet creation.

5 Use different-sized brushes, some sponges and even your fingers to paint your canvas carpet.

6 When you're done, let your carpet dry completely. It may take a day or two.

7 Apply one coat of acrylic varnish and let dry for a day. Apply a second coat and let dry.

Safety Note:

Always varnish your work in a well-ventilated area, wearing a safety mask and gloves. Set it outside to dry.

Terrific Techniques

Plop a few favorite colors onto a smooth surface such as paper or a prepared piece of canvas, wood or cardboard, and test out these techniques. Acrylic paints are your best bet because they can go from super-thick to wishy-washy with just a bit of water.

• Apply your paint thickly with a brush, palette knife or hand. This technique is called impasto.

• Scratch a painted surface with a stick, the end of your paintbrush or your fingernail to reveal the color of the paint underneath. This technique is called sgraffito.

• With your brush, drag dryish paint over another layer of paint so that the color underneath partially shows through. This technique is called scumbling.

Simple Stencils

Try a simple stencil when you want to paint a pattern that repeats. Here's how.

1 With an adult's help, use an X-Acto knife to cut out a simple design from bristol board or acetate.

2 Tape the stencil flat on whatever surface you want to decorate.

3 Mix your acrylic or latex paints. Try a few different tints, tones and shades of each color (see Creative Color Lab #4).

4 Use a rag, a sponge or a flat, round brush to daub or a toothbrush to spray your palette of colors over your stencil.

5 Move your stencil and repeat.

POSTCARDS FROM PARADISE

In the 1880s, some French painters filled their canvases with tiny dots of color. When you look at these paintings, your eyes blend the tiny dots together, making brilliant colors and amazing images. Use this technique to paint your own image of paradise and post it!

Artist's Tools

- white bristol board
- pencil, ruler, scissors
- fine-tip markers or Q-tips and acrylic paints
- waxed paper or palette

1 On the bristol board, measure rectangles for your postcards, about 15 cm x 10 cm (6 in. x 4 in.). Cut out the postcards.

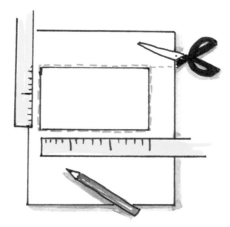

2 For your paradise, find a special scene — or imagine one. Your backyard? The beach? A holiday photograph?

3 Lightly sketch the scene on your postcard. Keep the image simple. Start with the background and work your way forward.

4 Using markers or a Q-tip dipped in acrylic paints, fill in your sketch by adding one dot of color at a time. This technique is called stippling.

● Start with the strongest or main color. If there's lots of grass in your scene, for example, start with green.

● Choose lighter shades of the same color and add highlights.

● Choose darker shades of the same color and add shadows.

● Choose complementary colors to make your postcard bold and brilliant. These colors are opposite each other on a color wheel.

● Adding dots of colors that seem very similar will make your paradise look soft and serene. These colors (called analogous colors) are next to each other on a color wheel.

Dazzling Duos

Experiment with complementary colors — red and green, blue and orange, yellow and violet. They can produce dazzling effects!

• Cut out orange flames from construction paper and glue them to a blue background. Combining warm colors (orange, yellow, red) with cool colors (blue, green, violet) will give your artwork lots of exciting energy.

• Brush your favorite color onto a postcard-sized piece of paper in the form of a picture, design or word — like your name. Paint around it with the complementary color. Stare at your picture for about 30 seconds and close your eyes. Open them and look again. What do you see?

• If you mix complementary colors, all you'll get is gray.

CREATIVE COLOR LAB #8

Scenic Experiment

For this colorful experiment, you'll need drawing paper, markers, chalk pastels and two sheets of tracing paper.

1 With your markers and pastels, draw the background of a simple landscape.

2 Tape a sheet of tracing paper over your background. Add another layer of scenic details to the middle ground.

3 Place a second sheet of tracing paper on top of your drawing and add a few quick details to the foreground.

Notice how the colors covered up with the white tracing paper seem softer and farther away and how the stronger colors appear closer.

Try painting your scene without the tracing paper, using soft colors for the background and strong colors for the foreground.

BRIGHT SUMMER BOUQUET

The great outdoors is filled with inspiring images to paint or sketch. Take your art studio outside and create a colorful close-up of your favorite flower.

Artist's Tools

- flowers
- magnifying glass
- drawing board or easel
- paper, pencil and eraser
- chalk pastels
- tissue

1 Examine each part of your flower with a magnifying glass. How many shapes can you see? How many colors? What's the lightest color? What's the darkest color? Is anything living inside?

2 Choose a small section of your flower and lightly sketch the shapes you see.

3 Start with the chalk color that's closest to the lightest color in your flower. Press firmly, following the forms and shapes of your sketch.

4 Using a tissue, blend your chalk lines together. Be sure to follow the shapes of your flower.

5 Continue adding and blending the colors of your flower, working from lightest to darkest.

6 Add details last, such as bright yellow stamens in the center, veins in the petals or bold, beautiful bugs!

7 Make several studies of each flower part and put them together to create one enormous image!

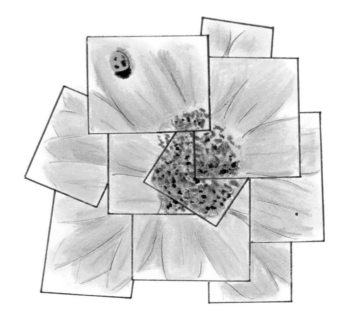

WINTER WONDERLAND

Create a snowy winter scene that's filled with colors that sparkle and shine in the sun.

Artist's Tools

- light blue or gray construction paper
- oil pastels
- white glue
- assortment of white collage materials, such as cotton balls, whipped cream, Model Magic, glue, paper, marshmallows
- scissors
- toothpick

1 Color the construction paper using a white oil pastel. Be sure to press firmly and fill in the page completely.

2 Glue a collage of winter-white materials to your white-covered construction paper. Here are some things to try:

- cotton-ball clouds
- paper-thin snowflakes
- marshmallow mountains or monsters

3 Use a toothpick, the tip of a safety pin or your fingernail to scratch some sketches onto your winter-white scene. Perky penguins? Tall trees? The gray or blue of the paper should show through.

4 Decide where the sun should be and draw it in with your pastels.

5 Use tiny amounts of different green, blue or violet pastels to gently blend in some cool, crisp shadows. Remember, shadows will fall in areas that are blocked from the sun.

6 Use tiny amounts of red, yellow or orange for finishing touches.

All Washed Up!

Watercolors have a nice wishy-washy character. Go with the flow!

Brush, sponge or spray your paper with water.

• Dip a wet brush or sponge in paint and add a coat of color.

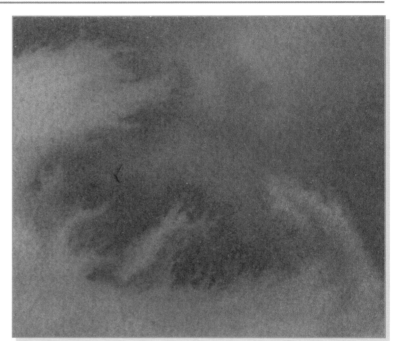

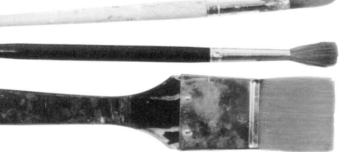

• Drip-drop wet paint and water for beautiful "blooms."

- Sprinkle on some rock salt and watch super stains appear.

- Brush watercolor over an image drawn with crayon or oil pastel for an ir*resist*ible effect.

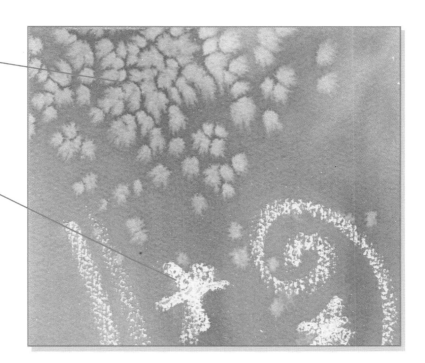

- When your painting is dry, dip a dry brush into wet watercolors and "drag" it across your colorful composition.

Artist's Tip:

Wet paint causes paper to bend and buckle. Tape the edges to a worktable with masking tape.

SWASHBUCKLING SEASCAPE

Stay afloat with this boatload of ideas for a spectacular watercolor seascape.

Artist's Tools

- watercolor paper or bristol board
- masking tape
- pencil and eraser
- paintbrushes
- container of water
- watercolors

1 Tape the edges of the watercolor paper to your worktable.

2 Lightly sketch the horizon at the upper or lower third of the page. This is where the sky and water meet.

3 What do you see in your seascape? A shipwreck? Whales? Palm trees? Lightly sketch some simple images and details.

4 Begin painting "wet on wet." Wet your page slightly by brushing water all the way across, from top to bottom.

• Dip a fat brush in water and then in the sky color. Start at the top of the page, brushing from side to side, moving down toward the horizon line. Brush around the objects or details in your sketch.

• Load your brush with the color of the water. Start at the bottom of the page, brushing from side to side, moving up toward the horizon line. Brush around the objects or details in your sketch. Let dry.

5 Choose the colors you want for the details in your seascape. Now get ready to paint "wet on dry."

• Load a fine-tip brush with paint and begin filling in details. Start with the background, move forward to the middle ground and finish with the details in the foreground.

• To make things seem farther away, dip your brush in water to lighten your colors.

• To make colors seem brighter and images appear closer, use a brush loaded with lots of paint (other than white).

Artist's Tip:

Before you start painting, test your brush on a piece of paper. Is your brush too wet? Too dry? Add more water or color as needed.

ALL WRAPPED UP

Cool curtains? A crazy costume? A treasured textile? Have some fun with food coloring and get all wrapped up in this fabric project! It calls for paper fabric, which is available in large rolls at most craft shops.

Artist's Tools

- old clothes and plastic gloves
- plastic sheet or garbage bags
- newspapers
- roll of paper fabric
- food coloring
- old plastic containers
- permanent or metallic markers
- spray bottle filled with water
- paintbrushes, all sizes
- string or elastics

1 Put on old clothes and spread a plastic sheet on the floor or table. Cover the sheet with newspapers. Unroll a long section of paper fabric on top of the newspapers.

2 Wearing gloves, mix your food coloring in old plastic containers. The more water you add, the lighter or softer the colors. Larger amounts of food coloring will create brighter, bolder colors.

3 If you like, draw some simple designs or images on your paper fabric using permanent or metallic markers.

4 Spray water on the fabric or dampen it by dipping it in a basin of water. This will help your colors spread.

5 Add some color.

• Use fat brushes to spread or splash on large areas of color.

• Use thin brushes for detailed marks and designs.

6 Try dunking small parts of the fabric into the food coloring.

7 Try twisting sections of your fabric, tying them with string or elastic and dipping them into the food coloring.

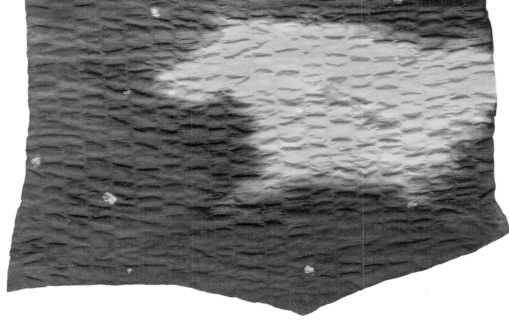

8 Hang your masterpiece outside to dry.

Printed Pictures

There are lots of printmaking techniques to try. Some are as simple as

• folding a blob of paint in a piece of paper

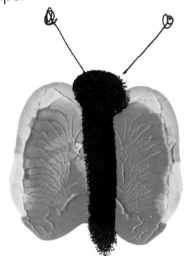

• leaving a trail of funny fingerprints behind

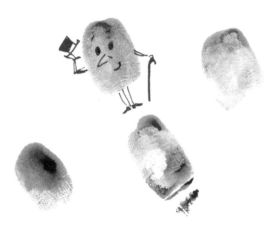

• pressing a piece of paper on top of a painted surface

Artist's Tip:

Dried prints make beautiful backgrounds for drawing images with chalk pastels or markers.

Letters and Numbers

A printed image appears reversed on the surface it's pressed onto, so you may need to do a little planning and preparation.

1 Use a metal nail file or a safety pin to carve your initials in a flat eraser, a potato, a bar of soap or a piece of thick Styrofoam.

2 Press the carved block into an ink pad and make a series of impressive prints on a piece of paper.

Helpful Hint!

Before you start carving, try drawing your initials on a piece of paper — reversed, of course! Hold the drawing in front of a mirror and check to see if its reflection is right.

MAKE A WISH!

Your wishes will come true if you let them fly! Make wish flags and offer them to the wind.

Artist's Tools

- scissors
- banner paper, a plastic-like paper found at art supply and craft stores
- newspapers
- acrylic paints or ink
- paper, pencil and eraser
- pieces of Styrofoam or Styrofoam meat trays
- paintbrush
- brayer or small paint roller
- twine
- clothespins or paper clips

1 Use sharp scissors to cut the sheet of banner paper into several small strips. Place them on old newpapers.

2 Stain the strips by brushing them with watery acrylic paints or ink. Let dry.

3 Sketch out a few ideas on paper. What does your wish look like? A smiling face? A heart-shaped bird? A secret symbol?

4 Using a pencil, draw three or four favorite ideas on separate pieces of Styrofoam. Press your pencil into the surface of the Styrofoam to create grooves.

5 Brush or roll your favorite color of ink or paint over each piece of Styrofoam. Don't add too much ink or paint — it shouldn't fill up the grooves of your wishful images.

6 Using the Styrofoam as printing blocks, press your designs onto the banner paper strips. Print all your strips.

7 Find a place outside and make a clothesline with the twine. Using clothespins or paper clips, hang up your beautiful printed wishes. Let them soar.

FLYING FISH

In this printmaking project, you get to turn your room into a silly school and teach some fish to fly.

Artist's Tools

- newspapers
- a plastic mesh bag (the kind onions or fruit come in)
- scraps of old, soft fabric
- acrylic paints
- plastic containers
- paintbrush
- newsprint paper (in an assortment of colors)
- markers
- chalk pastels or colored pencils.
- scissors
- masking tape

1 Cover your worktable with newspapers.

2 Mix some acrylic colors in plastic containers. Add just a little water — the paint shouldn't be either gloppy or runny.

3 Stuff your mesh bag with some soft fabric scraps and tie it closed. Lightly brush the "scaly" surface with paint or dip one part directly into the container of paint. (Be careful not to get too much paint on it or your print will be blotchy.)

4 Press the painted part of the mesh onto the piece of paper. Don't move it around too much or your print will end up fuzzy and blurred. Fill your page with scaly-looking prints.

5 Repeat steps 1 to 4 on several sheets of paper. Let dry.

6 With your markers and chalk pastels,

- sketch in fun fish shapes over top of your printed pages
- draw in details
- add colorful spots and stripes
- have a little fun with your fish

7 Let your fish fly! Cut out a few of your favorite fish and organize them into playful patterns by taping them to the wall or ceiling.

STARRY SKY

This mural will turn your room into a little bit of heaven. Tack it to the ceiling and take a trip to the stars.

Artist's Tools

- newspapers
- large piece of craft paper
- acrylic, tempera or finger paints
- pie plates
- paintbrushes
- star-shaped printing blocks, made from sponges, Styrofoam or potatoes
- slide projector and slides
- markers, chalk pastels or colored pencils

1 Cover the floor with newspapers and lay a long piece of craft paper on top.

2 Choose colors for your night sky. Brilliant blues? Deep violets? Plop the colors onto the paper, and use your hands or big brushes to mix, blend and spread the paint over the entire surface. Let dry.

3 Choose paint colors that contrast with your night sky, such as yellow, gold, silver and bronze acrylics. Mix the paints in pie plates.

4 Dip the star-shaped blocks into the paint and press them onto your night-sky background. Try splattering on some paint, too. Let dry.

5 Set up the slide projector at one end of your room opposite a wall large enough to hold your night-sky mural. (You can borrow a projector and slides of planets, animals or famous paintings from a library.)

6 Place your favorite slide in the projector and turn it on. The image will appear on the wall. Adjust the size of the image by moving the projector back and forth.

7 When your mural is dry, tack it to the wall that your image is projected on and trace what you see.

- Use metallic markers to outline shapes.
- Use chalk pastels to fill in spaces.
- Use paints to brush on a bit more color.

What starry constellations appear in your night sky?

Transforming Ideas into Sculptures

Propel your ideas into the third dimension!
Sculpture is the art of transforming ideas
into objects you can walk — or fly —
all the way around!

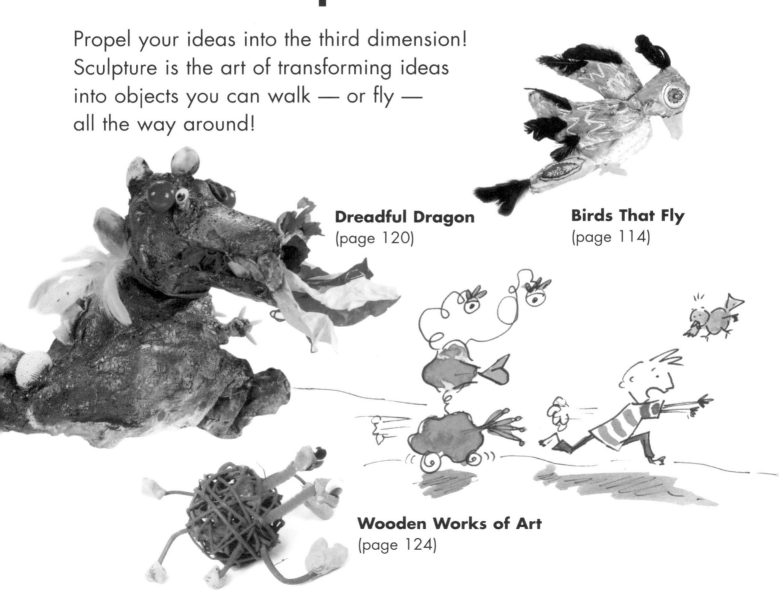

Dreadful Dragon
(page 120)

Birds That Fly
(page 114)

Wooden Works of Art
(page 124)

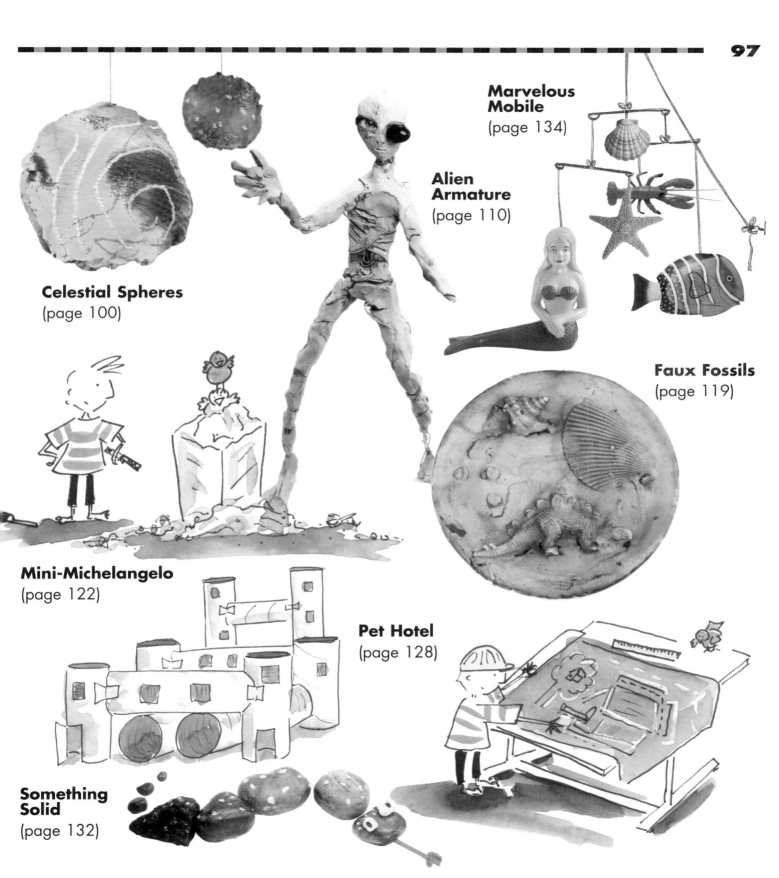

Marvelous Mobile
(page 134)

Alien Armature
(page 110)

Celestial Spheres
(page 100)

Faux Fossils
(page 119)

Mini-Michelangelo
(page 122)

Pet Hotel
(page 128)

Something Solid
(page 132)

In the Sculpture Studio

Here are some tools and materials to help get some of
your best 3-dimensional ideas off the ground.

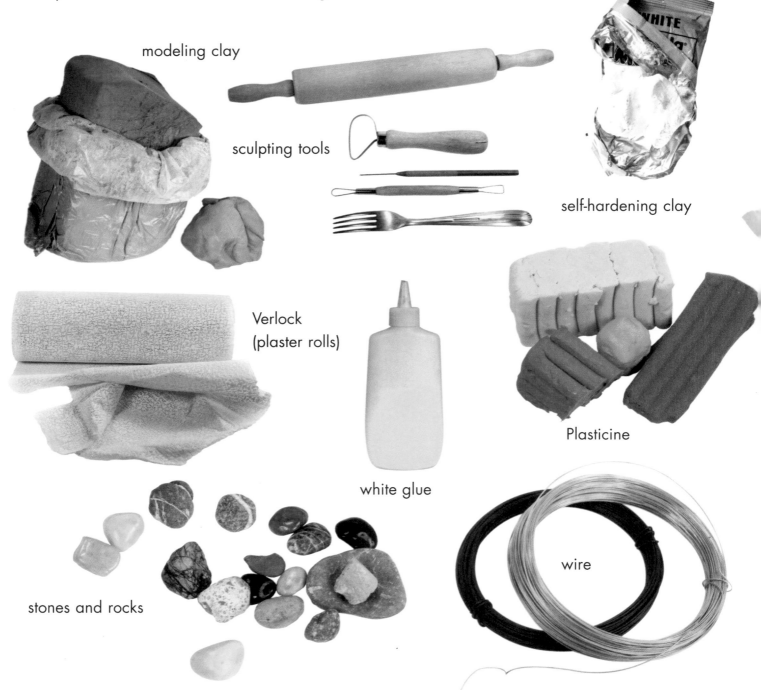

modeling clay

sculpting tools

self-hardening clay

Verlock
(plaster rolls)

white glue

Plasticine

stones and rocks

wire

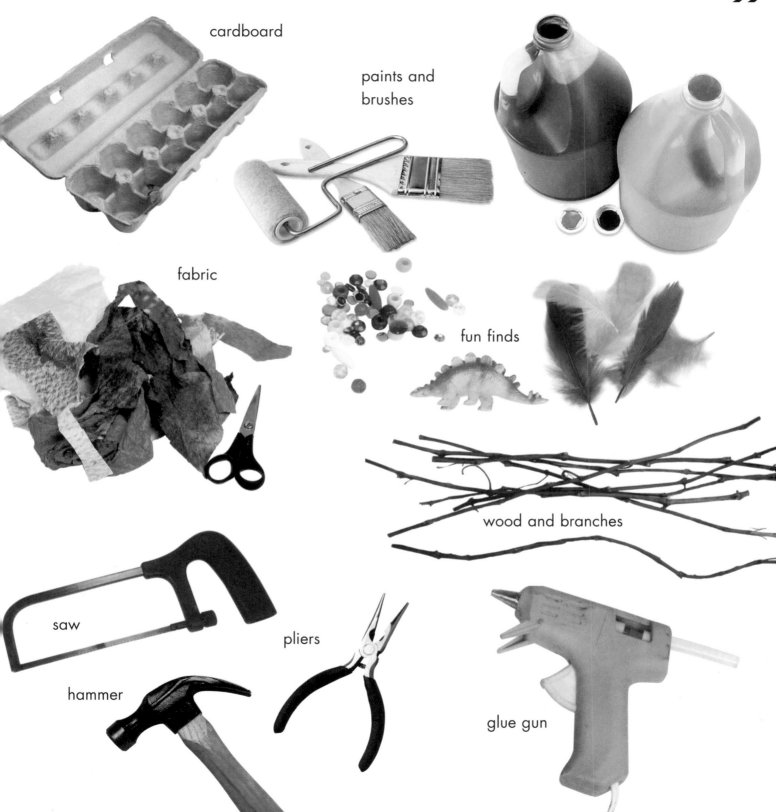

cardboard

paints and brushes

fabric

fun finds

wood and branches

saw

pliers

hammer

glue gun

CELESTIAL SPHERES

Create a mini solar system from just a few materials. Hang this spacey soft sculpture from your ceiling.

Artist's Tools

- paper fabric
- pencil
- scissors
- newspapers
- food coloring
- paintbrushes
- acrylic metallic paints or glitter
- needle and thread
- cotton batting or foam chips
- tape

1 To make planets and the Sun, cut a few folded paper fabric pieces into different-sized circles. For perfect circles, trace around different-sized dinner plates or other large, round objects.

2 Lay the circles on newspapers. Brush on some food coloring (see pages 86–87 for some ideas on mixing and painting with food coloring). Let dry.

3 Make your spheres sparkle. Brush on some metallic paint to add a few highlights (or use glue and glitter). Let dry.

4 Place two circles together, with the painted sides on the inside. Sew around the outside, about 1 cm (½ in.) from the edge. Leave a 7 cm (3 in.) hole on one side for adding the stuffing.

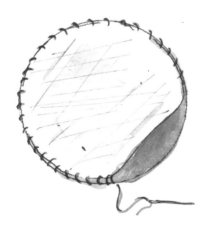

5 Turn your spheres right side out. Stuff them with cotton batting or foam chips. Sew up the stuffing holes.

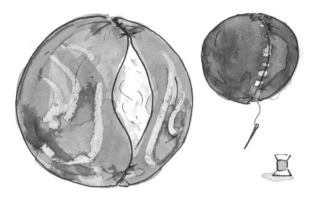

6 Stitch a long piece of thread through the tops of your spheres and tape them to your ceiling.

A STAR IS BORN

Use your imagination to create some spectacular stars. Then hang them from the ceiling along with your celestial spheres. Or make a magic wand and presto! You've just created a super star!

Artist's Tools

- self-hardening clay
- fun finds (pipe cleaners, wire mesh, straws, foil, etc.)
- glue and glitter
- acrylic metallic paints and brushes, metallic markers
- thread or chopsticks
- tape

1 Make some star shapes out of the clay.

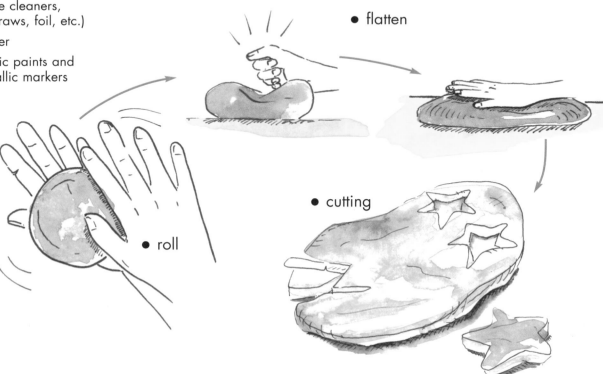

- flatten
- roll
- cutting

2 Don't forget to make a hole!

- Poke a small hole in the tops of your stars if you want to hang them up.

- Stick them on the end of chopsticks for a standing sculpture.

3 Glue on or press in some fun finds.

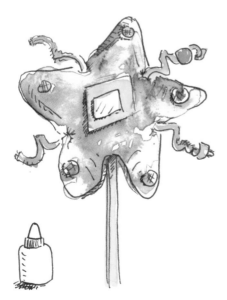

4 Let your stars dry and decorate them with

- metallic paints
- markers
- glue and glitter

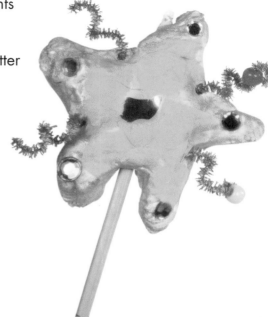

5 Hang some stars up (when dry) by stringing thread through the hole and taping them to your ceiling.

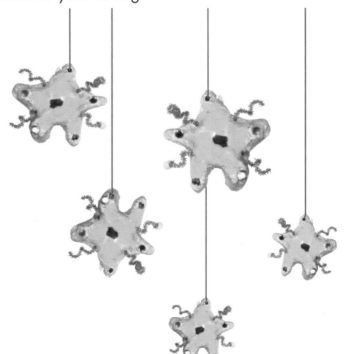

CREATING WITH CLAY

Create some fantastic forms out of clay. Once you know a few simple secrets about working with clay, you can make almost anything. Sculpt an ancient pot or a mighty mastodon — or even a sloppy sandwich!

Buying Clay

Many craft or art supply stores sell two kinds of clay.

- There's self-hardening or self-drying clay that comes in small packages.

- And there's clay that comes in 14–23 kg (30–50 lb.) bags or boxes. This is the clay that many potters and sculptors use, and it's usually dried in a kiln (see page 107). **Beware:** A bag of this clay is really heavy, so make sure you have some help lifting it and getting it home.

Clay-Sculpting Tools

You can buy tools for working with clay at craft or art supply stores, but you can also improvise with things around the house. You'll be using these tools for scraping, cutting, rolling, smoothing, wetting and shaping.

Getting Started

- Cover your work area. Wet clay sticks itself silly to any smooth surface. It's best to use a piece of heavy canvas cloth.

- Cut your clay. Use a string or thin wire to cut a small piece of clay off your big hunk.

- Wedge your clay. Wedging is just like kneading a piece of dough, except it requires a little more muscle. Wedging removes any air bubbles trapped inside the clay before you begin. If your clay sculpture has air bubbles inside, it might crack or break.

Sculpting Techniques

Try some of these techniques for shaping and forming your clay.

- **Pinch:** Use your fingers to pinch out a shape, form or design.

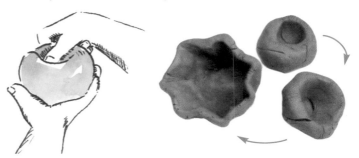

- **Coil:** Roll your clay into long snakes and then layer them on top of one another. They can be smoothed or blended together.

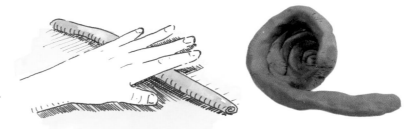

- **Slab:** Flatten your clay with a rolling pin, but not too thin. Cut it into slabs that you can attach or join together.

Attaching Clay Pieces

Here's how to join pieces of clay together so all your carefully sculpted parts don't fall off.

● **Score:** Use a fork to score, or scratch, the surface of each piece you want to join together. The grooves shouldn't be too deep.

● **Slip:** This is the soft, slippery stuff that will stick your pieces together. To make slip, just add lots of water to a bit of clay and mix it up. Use a finger or Popsicle stick to apply the slip to the scored parts of the clay. Press the "slipped" pieces together and smooth the joined parts over with your finger or stick.

Drying Clay

Let your clay sculpture dry slowly to prevent crumbling, cracking and curling.

● Wrap your clay sculpture in a damp cheesecloth or loose plastic bag. When most of the moisture is gone, set it in a warm place.

● Set flat clay pieces on a screen or rack so that enough air gets underneath.

I'm a little teapot, short and stout ...

Firing Clay

If you use the kind of clay that potters use, your sculpture will need to be fired in a kiln. A kiln is a special kind of oven or furnace that is used to heat clay and ceramic pieces to very high temperatures to get rid of every bit of moisture. To find a kiln you can use, try your local community center or potter's studio.

When your clay has been fired once, or "bisque fired," it is ready to be glazed or painted.

kiln

bisque-fired clay sculpture

Glazing Clay

Glazes are special paints potters use to add color to their creations. Ask for help finding the right glazes at pottery supply shops. Once you have glazed your pottery, it must go back in the kiln for a second firing, or "glaze firing."

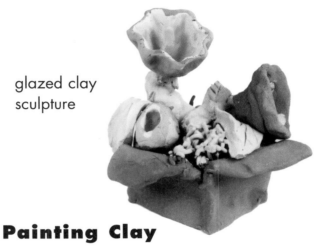

glazed clay sculpture

Painting Clay

If you don't fire your clay or are using self-hardening clay, you can use acrylic paints, India ink or even shoe polish to add color to your clay creations once they are dry.

DOWN TO EARTH

Create a clay landscape and fill it with some down-to-earth creatures. A forest full of trolls? A Stone-Age cave? A medieval moat?

Artist's Tools

- large piece of self-hardening clay
- cloth or canvas to cover worktable
- fun finds (pipe cleaners, paper scraps, toys, etc.)
- toothpicks
- piece of wire mesh or garlic press
- acrylic paints

Creating Features

Can you work all of these techniques, forms and features into your landscape?

1 Flatten a chunk of your clay to about 5 cm (2 in.) thick.

2 Divide it into hills and valleys by pushing and pinching with your thumb and fingers.

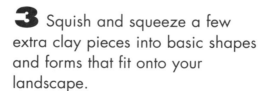

3 Squish and squeeze a few extra clay pieces into basic shapes and forms that fit onto your landscape.

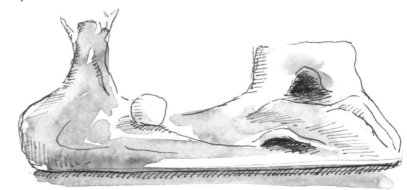

4 Expand your ideas by pressing in a few fun finds.

5 Add some texture by perforating or poking holes into your clay pieces with a toothpick. Or try pressing clay through a wire mesh or garlic press.

6 Roll some clay pieces into long snaky strips and make a maze or rolling river.

7 Brighten up your landscape with some acrylic paint.

Creating Creatures

Create the creatures that live in your landscape with extra bits of clay, or use old toys.

Spectacular Sculptures

Try rolling, pinching, cutting or pressing clay through a garlic press.

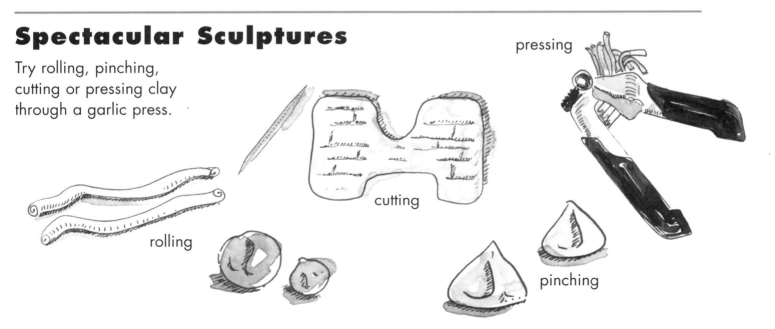

pressing

cutting

rolling

pinching

ALIEN ARMATURE

An armature is like a sculpture's skeleton. Without one, some aliens haven't got a leg to stand on!

- safety goggles and gloves
- wire that's bendable and holds a shape
- self-hardening clay or Plasticine

1 Wearing the goggles and gloves, make a wiry figure by

- bending

- twisting

- shaping

- trying all sorts of positions

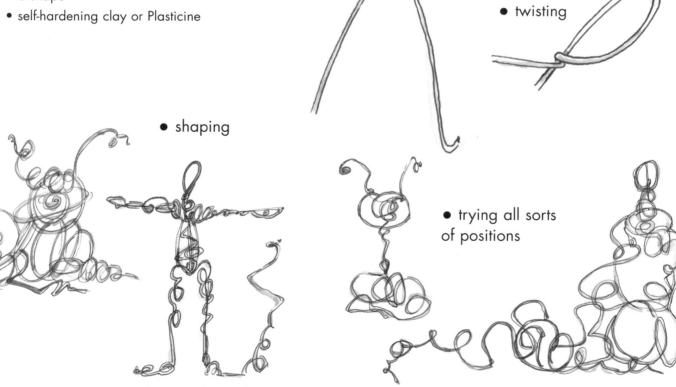

2 Give your figure some alien body parts using pieces of clay. You don't need to cover the whole armature.

3 Add some interesting details.

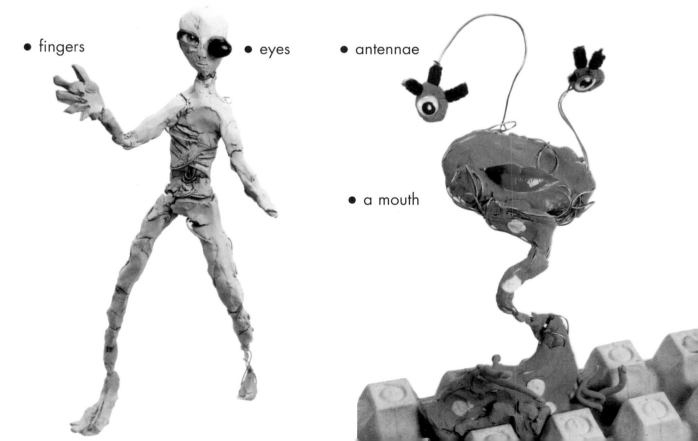

- fingers
- eyes
- antennae
- a mouth

MAGIC CARPET

Artists have been weaving stories into wall hangings, called tapestries, for hundreds of years. In this soft-sculpture project, you get to weave your favorite fantasy into a magic carpet.

Artist's Tools

- old bed sheet or paper fabric
- newspapers
- food coloring
- paintbrushes
- scissors
- masking tape
- fun finds (buttons, fake fur, feathers, sticks, tiny toys, rope, ribbon, etc.)
- needle and thread

1 Cover your worktable with newspapers and spread out the old sheet or paper fabric. Brush on some color (see pages 86–87 for tips on transforming a plain piece of fabric). Let dry.

2 Cut 5 or 6 long strips, 5 cm (2 in.) wide and 1 m (1 yd.) long. Cut 15 to 20 shorter strips, 5 cm (2 in.) wide and 60 cm (2 ft.) long.

3 Attach one end of the long strips to your worktable with masking tape, leaving about 5 cm (2 in.) between each one. Add some long strips of fun finds (ribbon, fake fur, tin foil, streamers) before you start weaving.

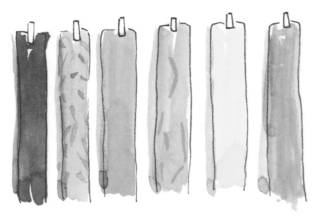

4 Weave the short strips over and under the long strips. The first short strip starts over the first long strip, and the next short strip starts under the first long strip. Keep alternating.

5 Sew along the outside edges of your carpet so that all the strips are secure.

6 Add anything that strikes your fancy.

- Twist in some pipe cleaners.
- Glue on some glitter.
- Tie on a tiny toy.
- Sew on a beautiful button.

BIRDS THAT FLY

Let your imagination take flight with this soft-sculpture bird. Create a whole flock that swoops and soars from your ceiling.

Artist's Tools

- marker and sheets of newspaper
- meter (yard) of fabric for one bird
- chalk
- scissors
- needle and thread
- foam chips or cotton batting
- markers
- glue gun
- Model Magic
- fun finds (feathers, beads, foil, etc.)
- fabric paint

2 Fold the fabric in half, with the right side of the fabric on the inside. Place your pattern pieces on the fabric so that the top of the bird's head and the part of the wing that attaches to the body are on the fold.

1 Use a marker and sheets of newspaper to make a pattern of a bird's body and half of a wing. Carefully cut out the pattern pieces.

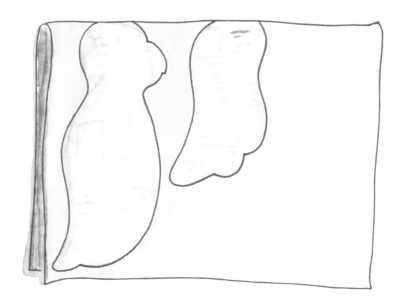

3 Using chalk, outline the bird's body. Outline the wing pattern twice. Cut the pieces out. Do not cut along the fold.

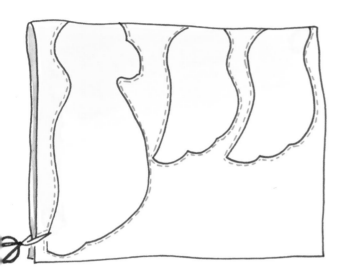

4 With the right sides together, sew or glue around the bird's body, about 2.5 cm (1 in.) from the edge. Leave a 10 cm (4 in.) hole on one side for adding the stuffing. Have an adult help if you are using a glue gun.

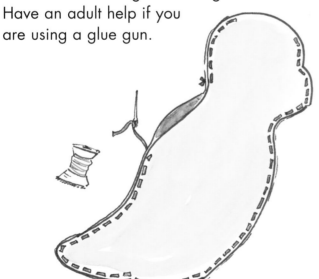

5 Open up the wings and place one on top of the other, right sides together. Sew around the wings, about 2.5 cm (1 in.) from the edge. Leave a stuffing hole on one side.

6 Turn the fabric pieces right side out, and stuff the body and wings with foam chips or cotton batting.

7 Sew up the stuffing holes, and stitch the wings to the body.

8 Glue on a beak made of fabric or Model Magic.

9 Add some fanciful fun finds and dab on some fabric paint.

CREATING WITH PLASTER

Plaster is a great material for transforming your ideas into three dimensions. Carve a crazy gargoyle! Make fabulous fake fossils!

Tips from Plaster Masters

• Always wear a safety mask over your nose and mouth when mixing and working with plaster to avoid inhaling plaster dust. It's a good idea to wear gloves, too.

• Add goggles when you're carving and sculpting plaster.

• Wet plaster dries very quickly. Get everything ready before you start mixing.

• Grease your face and other body parts with petroleum jelly before sticking them in wet plaster or applying plaster strips.

• Don't pour wet plaster down the drain. When it dries, it will clog things up permanently.

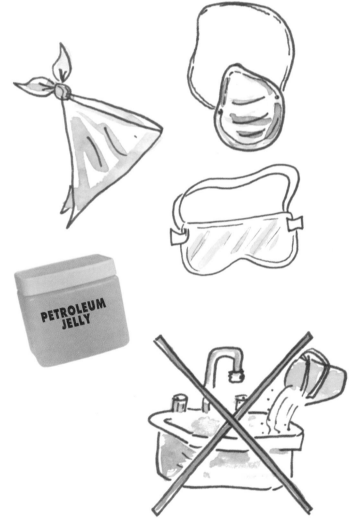

Buying Plaster

Plaster is a soft, white powder made from a mineral called gypsum.

• You can buy boxes or bags of plaster (sometimes called plaster of paris) in most art supply shops, craft and hardware stores.

• Many craft stores also sell plaster strips or big rolls of cheesecloth covered with plaster (called Verlock).

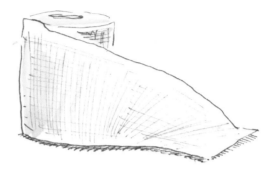

Mixing Plaster

1 Put on a safety mask and rubber gloves. Find an old bucket, an old bowl, a wooden spoon or stick, and a measuring cup.

2 Pour 250 ml (1 c.) of warm water into the bucket.

3 Measure 500 ml (2 c.) of plaster into an old bowl or other container.

4 Add the plaster to the water, one handful at a time. Keep mixing as you're adding.

5 When making larger or smaller amounts of plaster, always use twice as much plaster as water in your mixture.

Molding Plaster

Now the fun begins!

1 Find or make some shapes, or molds, to pour your plaster into — old cake pans or muffin trays, jelly molds, boxes or plastic containers.

2 Cover your work surface with a large piece of cardboard or plastic. Place your mold on top, and pour your plaster carefully into the mold. Let dry and remove the mold.

Painting Plaster

• When dry, plaster creations can be brushed with acrylic paints.

Adding and Subtracting

• Add things to the wet plaster to express your best artistic ideas — sticks, shells, jewels, Plasticine shapes, handprints, etc.

• Subtract parts of your finished plaster piece. Carve hills and valleys or noble noses using a spoon, a Popsicle stick or a plastic knife. The plaster is soft so you don't need a sharp carving tool.

Faux Fossils

1 Firmly press a chunk of modeling clay into the bottom of an old plastic bowl or container.

2 Press a few fun objects like shells or small plastic animals, dinosaurs, cars or people into the clay. Remove your fun objects from the clay, making sure they leave a clear imprint.

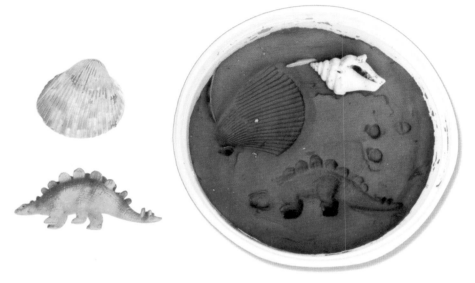

3 Pour the wet plaster mixture into the plastic container, completely covering your imprinted clay with an inch or two of wet plaster.

4 When the plaster has completely hardened, pop it out of the container.

DREADFUL DRAGON

Wrap some plaster strips around a stuffed form and create a dreadful dragon. Or a gruesome giant. Or a handsome swan.

Artist's Tools

- plastic bags and newspapers
- masking tape
- scissors
- cardboard tubes, egg cartons, pieces of foam, Plasticine, Popsicle sticks
- roll of plaster (Verlock)
- bowl
- acrylic paints and brushes
- glitter, sequins, sea salt, sand, etc.
- glue gun

Make a Form

1 Stuff three plastic bags with newspaper: one for the head, one for the body, one for the tail.

2 Wrap each part with masking tape to create the right shape. Use more tape to attach the separate parts.

3 Use pieces of foam, cardboard tubes, egg cartons, Popsicle sticks, Plasticine and anything else that works to make dragon features — a snout, horns, wings, teeth, claws. Attach the features to the dragon form with masking tape.

Plaster It

4 Cut short strips from the plaster roll.

5 Dip one strip at a time into a container of water. The strip needs to be wet but not sopping.

6 One by one, spread the strips over the dragon form and features until everything is completely covered. Let dry.

Dress It Up

7 Brush on some color. Green skin? Yellow scales? Red spots?

8 While the paint is still wet, sprinkle on glitter, sequins, sea salt or sand.

9 When the dragon is dry, have an adult help you use a glue gun to add some character. Jewels? Crazy eyeballs? A blaze of flames?

MINI-MICHELANGELO

Michelangelo was a master sculptor and painter in Italy in the 1500s. Put on your goggles and gloves, and get ready to carve your own monumental ideas into a one-of-a-kind sculpture.

Artist's Tools

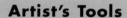

- safety mask, goggles and gloves
- sawdust
- plaster powder
- large plastic container
- wooden spoon or paint stick
- empty 2 L (2 qt.) milk carton
- carving tools (plastic knife, spoon, sandpaper, nail file)

1 Wearing your mask, goggles and gloves, mix equal parts of sawdust and plaster powder in the plastic container.

2 Stir in just enough water to turn the mixture into thick gravy.

3 Pour the mixture into the milk carton. Let dry. (The plaster hardens quickly.)

4 After about an hour, the mixture will be solid. Tear off the milk carton.

5 Use some simple carving tools to

- cut
- scratch
- dig
- chip
- chisel
- sand

Breaking Points

- Your sculpture might topple if you chip or chisel too much.

- Your block might break if you dig too deep.

WOODEN WORKS OF ART

Wood comes in all sorts of shapes, sizes and forms that can be glued, nailed or bent into shape. You won't have to look far to find wonderful pieces to inspire your artistic ideas. Let the shape, size and texture of your wood lead the way!

Toothpicks and Popsicle Sticks

Add a bit of glue to these pieces of wood, and start scaling the heights. Don't forget to keep your balance.

Sticks and Branches

Twigs and sticks that are still green inside can be bent, twisted or tied into wonderfully warped shapes. Look for pieces that have already fallen to the ground — never cut branches from a living tree.

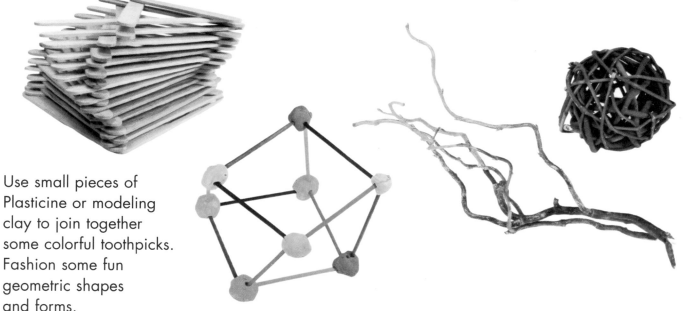

Use small pieces of Plasticine or modeling clay to join together some colorful toothpicks. Fashion some fun geometric shapes and forms.

The Woodpile

Check out the woodpile in your backyard, ask for leftover pieces of wood at building supply stores or search the beach for driftwood. Ask an adult to help you with sawing, nailing or drilling.

Balsa Wood

Balsa wood comes in long, thin pieces that you can cut into shapes with scissors and attach with glue. You'll find it in craft and hobby shops.

Finishing Your Sculptures

• Smooth things over with sandpaper.

• Paint all or parts of your sculpture with acrylic paint. Use watered-down acrylic paints for a colorful stained effect.

• Brush on an acrylic varnish or wood stain to bring out all the wonders of your wood. Attach fun finds like wire, pipe cleaners or beads.

ALIVE ART

Create a living sculpture that will grow and grow and grow.

Artist's Tools

- large plant pot filled with soil
- branches, garden sticks, bamboo poles, scraps of wood
- glue gun
- twine or wire
- safety goggles and gloves, if needed
- rocks
- acrylic paints, brushes
- climbing vine

1 Look around at nature for some free-flowing ideas for your sculpture.

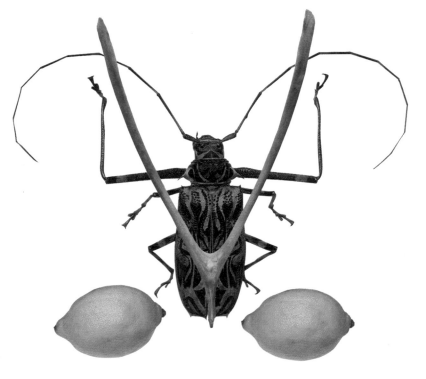

2 Make your structure stable.

- With an adult's help, glue the base of your structure to the outside of the pot.

- Crisscross twine or wire in and around the sticks, poles or branches. Wear goggles and gloves if you're working with wire.

- Keep your structure from wobbling or falling down by attaching extra sticks on top or rocks at the bottom.

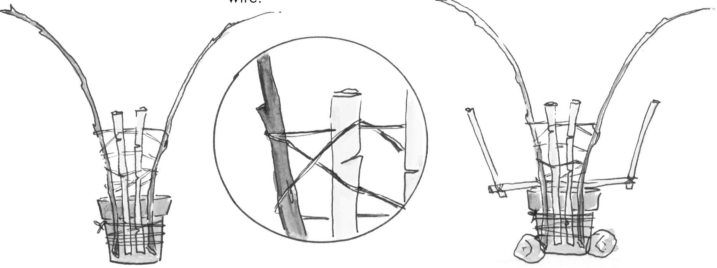

3 Brush your branches, sticks or poles with color.

- Use watered-down acrylic paint for soft stains.

- Try dots of pure color for highlights.

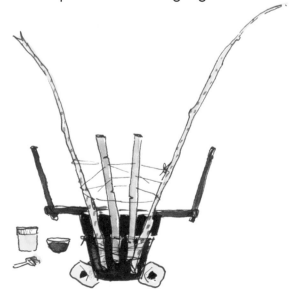

4 Plant your plant. Train the ends of the plant to grow up and around your structure.

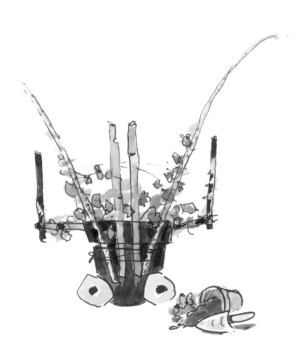

PET HOTEL

Be an artistic architect. Design and build a place for your favorite pet (real or imaginary) to roam around and hide in.

Successful Design

To create a successful design, architects have to think about function, form and materials.

1 Consider some questions:

- How big is your pet?

- What kind of environment is your pet happiest in?

- How much space do you have to work with?

- What construction materials do you have on hand?

2 Sketch some ideas.

- Start with some dream designs.

- Turn your best dream design into a practical plan.

Four-Star Habitats

Here are a few ideas for some artistic abodes for all sorts of pets.

Cardboard cat hotel

Classic canine canopy

Ladybug haven

Mouse mansion

ARTISTIC ASSEMBLAGE

Turn an old pile of junk into an artistic assemblage — which is just a 3-D form of collage. Some artists create amazing assemblages by putting found objects together in a new and surprising way.

1 Look for some interesting found objects

- inside the closet
- in the garage
- under the steps
- at a flea market

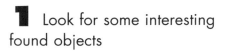

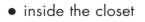

2 If you like, decorate your objects with acrylic paint or glue on some magazine cut-outs. Then assemble your objects in an original way.

What do you think of these artistic assemblages?

SOMETHING SOLID

Every stone has something to say about Earth's ancient history. Collect some stones and rocks that "speak" to you and make something that will stand the test of time.

1 Look for stones or rocks with interesting shapes, forms, marks, fossils or colors.

2 Try mixing, matching and balancing the color, form and weight of your stones.

Inukshuk

An inukshuk is a rock pile traditionally built by Native people of the Far North as a landmark for guiding their way home or marking a special place.

Rock Pile

Use acrylic paints to add color to rocks.

Precious Gems

Decorate yourself! Combine your rock collection with fun finds such as feathers, shells, washers and other pieces of hardware. Then use glue or thin wire from a jewelry kit or a craft store to attach your dramatic rock designs to ribbons, safety pins or leather strips.

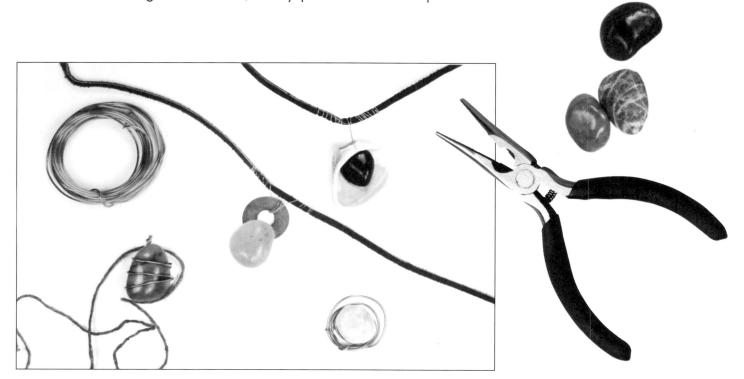

MARVELOUS MOBILE

Use your imaginative energy to make a mobile that will keep your 3-D forms bobbing, swaying and spinning in space.

Artist's Tools

- two hooks or eyelets
- string
- four or five wire clothes hangers
- wire cutters
- pliers
- broken toys and other favorite small objects

Create a Pulley

1 Attach a hook or eyelet to a good spot in the ceiling, not too close to the walls.

2 Loop a long piece of string through the hook or eyelet, letting one end dangle where you can reach it.

3 Tie the other end to another hook screwed into a nearby wall.

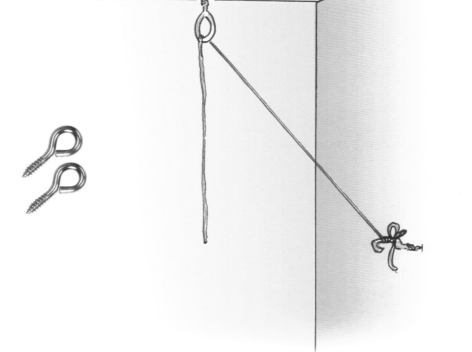

Make a Mobile

1 With an adult's help, cut out the bottoms of the wire hangers.

2 Use pliers to curl the ends into small hooks or loops.

3 Tie the dangling end of the string to the center of the first piece of wire.

4 Tie two different lengths of string to each end.

5 Tie the end of each piece of string to the center of two more wires.

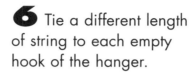

6 Tie a different length of string to each empty hook of the hanger.

7 Tie the toys and small objects to the string ends.

Balance Things Out

The weight of carefully balanced objects will keep your marvelous mobile moving.

Pull It Up

When your mobile is finished, send it up over your head and tie it off at a good height.

Mixing up your Media

You can combine your drawing, painting and sculpting materials and techniques in lots of wonderful ways. Mix up your media and transform what you see, feel and think into a world that reflects the real you!

Dangling DNA
(page 142)

Funny Faces
(page 145)

Wild-Thing Puppet
(page 168)

Whistling Ocarina
(page 162)

Recycled Robot
(page 188)

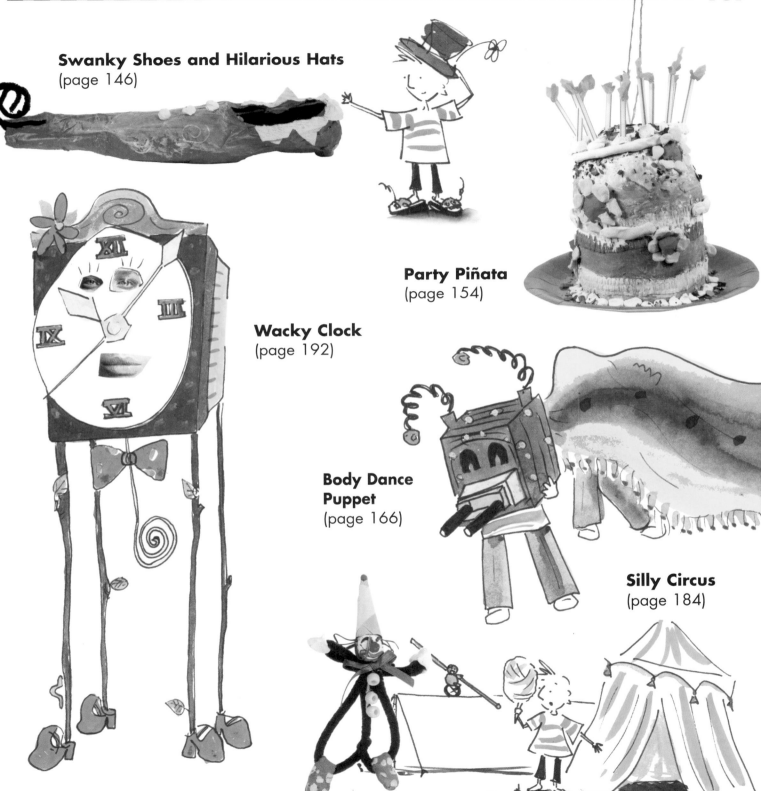

Swanky Shoes and Hilarious Hats
(page 146)

Party Piñata
(page 154)

Wacky Clock
(page 192)

**Body Dance
Puppet**
(page 166)

Silly Circus
(page 184)

In the Mixed-Media Studio

You'll have most materials already on hand, but here are a few more you might want to stick in a corner of your studio.

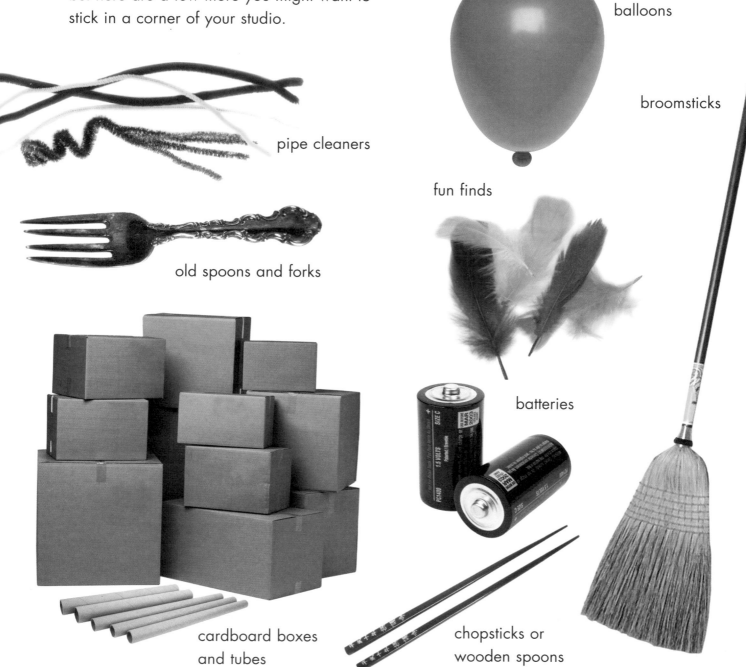

pipe cleaners

balloons

broomsticks

fun finds

old spoons and forks

batteries

cardboard boxes and tubes

chopsticks or wooden spoons

copper pipe and other hardware finds

toys

fabric scraps

clay pots

electrical wire

clock parts

old hats and shoes

small lightbulbs

CLEAR HUMAN BODY

Ever wonder what you're made of? Make a clear human body and learn to look at yourself from the inside out!

Artist's Tools

- large sheet of acetate or craft paper
- masking tape
- markers or acrylic paints
- glue
- body parts: Model Magic, string, pipe cleaners, balloons, sponges, telephone wire, Popsicle sticks, toothpicks, cardboard, construction paper, etc.
- anatomy book (optional)

1 Tape a life-sized sheet of acetate or craft paper to the floor. (If you want the body to be a miniature version of you, tape a smaller sheet of acetate or paper to a table.)

2 Lie down on the acetate or paper and have a friend outline your body with a marker. Or draw your own miniature body on the smaller sheet.

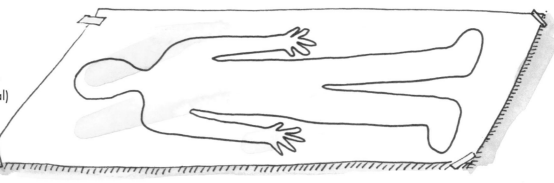

3 Time to test your anatomy know-how.

- Start with your big balloon heart.

- Glue down some strong Popsicle stick bones.

- Organize your sponge-like organs.

- Cut out your construction paper muscles.

- Attach your stringy arteries, veins and nerves.

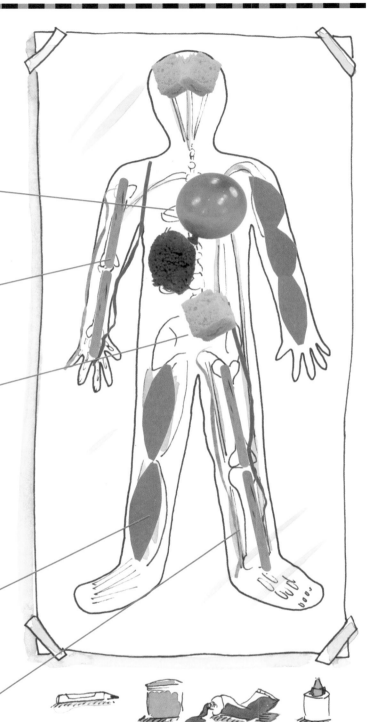

4 Use markers or acrylic paints to add some color and detail.

DANGLING DNA

DNA is the material in your genes that makes you a one-of-a-kind masterpiece. String together a collection of personal objects that shows off your unique character.

Artist's Tools

- collection of personal objects
- craft paper, acetate, old cards, etc.
- scissors
- glue
- hole punch
- ribbon, string, yarn, pipe cleaners, safety pins, paper clips, etc.

Collect Yourself

Search high and low for a collection of things that make up the real you: family photos, favorite drawings, handprints, small toys, jewelry, keys, tickets, bookmarks, hair ribbon, baby booties, baseball cards, valuable valentines, etc.

Suit Yourself

Glue or pin fragile objects or drawings to pieces of craft paper, acetate, old cards, etc. Cut them to a size and shape that suits you.

Connect Yourself

Make a hole in the top, sides or bottom of your photos, cards, drawings, etc. Then connect all of your collection with string, ribbon, yarn, pipe cleaners, safety pins, paper clips, etc.

Install Yourself

Find a good place to dangle your DNA:

- from a wall
- around your door
- from the ceiling

PORTRAIT GALLERY

Mix up your media and create a gallery of picture-perfect portraits of yourself.

Blind Contour Creation

Keep your eyes on yourself in a mirror and pen a portrait without looking at your page. Try this one using an ink pen and pastels on a brown paper bag.

Flower Power

How would you look if all your features were made from your favorite flowers? Collect an assortment of real or fake flowers and arrange them into a beautiful bouquet that resembles your reflection.

Funny Faces

Tack on some funny features and then spin them into different expressions.

1 Decorate a piece of cardboard with paints and markers.

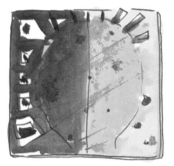

2 Cut out several different-sized shapes from the construction paper.

3 Use the thumb tacks or pushpins to attach the paper cut-outs to your decorated cardboard. See how many different faces you can make with these moveable features.

SWANKY SHOES AND HILARIOUS HATS

Get all dressed up and turn yourself into a work of art.

1 Get out your sketchbook and design some outrageous shoes and hats.

2 Scrunch up newspaper into the shapes or forms of your designs, and tape them to your shoes and hat.

3 Tear sheets of newspaper into lots of short strips, about 5 cm (2 in.) wide.

4 In a large bowl, mix the wallpaper paste with water, following the instructions on the box. Dip the newspaper strips into the paste mixture and spread them, one at a time, onto your shoes and hat. Let dry. Add another layer of papier-mâché. Let dry.

5 Paint your shoes and hat with acrylic colors.

6 Glue on fun finds for finishing touches. Have an adult help if you use a glue gun.

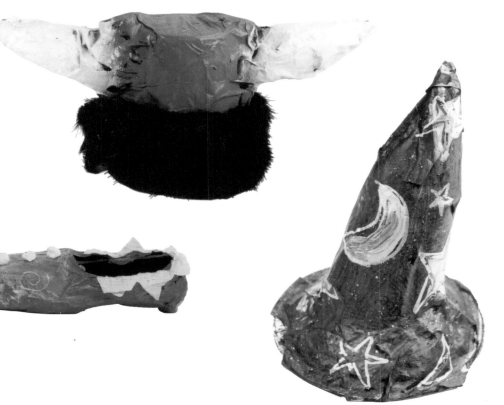

COOL COSTUMES

Costume designers use heaps of imagination and lots of artistic know-how to create cool costumes that capture special personalities.

Artist's Tools

- pencil and sketchbook
- tape measure
- markers
- newspaper
- scissors
- white cotton fabric or old bedsheet
- straight pins
- big garbage bag or sheet of plastic
- rubber gloves
- old clothes
- small plastic containers
- food coloring or fabric dyes
- paintbrushes, sponges, rags
- fabric glue or needle and thread
- fun finds (old ties, fabric scraps, buckles, belt, feathers, ribbon, beads, buttons, etc.)

Designing a Costume

Decide on a theme for your costume. Court jester? Wicked wizard? It's a good idea to start with some rough sketches.

Making a Pattern

1 Take some body measurements — your length, your width and your head size.

2 Tape some newspapers together so you can make your pattern life sized. Draw the pattern on the paper and cut it out.

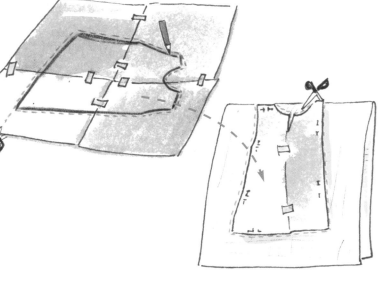

3 Fold the fabric in half. Place the pattern on the fabric with the top along the fold. Pin it in place and cut it out. Cut a small slit in the neck if the hole is tight for your head.

Creative Coloring

4 Put on old clothes and rubber gloves. Spread garbage bags or a plastic sheet over your work area. Spread your fabric on top.

5 Mix the food coloring or fabric dyes with water in plastic containers.

6 Use brushes, sponges or rags to paint your fabric. Hang to dry.

Fashionable Finishing

7 If you want side seams, sew or glue the seams together. Just make sure you leave holes for your arms.

8 Sew or glue on some fashionable fun finds.

MASQUERADE MASK

What kind of mask would be the perfect disguise for your personality? A sun god? A grizzly bear? A medieval knight? This is a great project to share with a friend. Ask an adventurous adult to help!

Artist's Tools

- pencil and sketchbook
- roll of plaster tape (for one mask)
- scissors
- headband or bandanna
- petroleum jelly
- mirror
- plastic container filled with warm water
- tissues
- newspapers
- hole punch
- scissors
- elastic, ribbon or string
- cardboard tubes, sponges, paper towels, Plasticine or Model Magic, fun finds, etc.
- acrylic paints and brushes

Designing Your Mask

In your sketchbook, draw a few different kinds of masks. Try some half-masks as well as full-face ones. What special features are part of your disguise? A unicorn horn? Nose warts? Glittery jewels?

Getting Ready

1 Cut a pile of plaster strips, each about 2.5 cm (1 in.) by 10 cm (4 in.).

2 Use a headband or a bandanna to hold your hair off your face. Smear petroleum jelly all over your face. Don't get it in your eyes.

3 Park yourself in front of a mirror with the pile of plaster strips, a container of warm water and tissues (for wiping drips) close by.

Molding Your Mask

Here's how to make a plaster mold of your face — the first step in creating a great mask. Once you (or a friend) start applying the strips, you'll have to keep a straight face — no moving or giggling!

1 Dip the plaster strips one at a time into the container of warm water. They should be wet, but not soaking.

2 For a full-face mask, apply the first strips on your forehead and then your cheeks and chin. For a half-face mask, apply the strips to your forehead, cheeks and nose. Be sure the side of the strips with the most plaster goes on the outside. Smooth each strip with your fingers so that it's molded to your face.

Safety Note:

Try a wet plaster strip on the back of your hand first. If your skin becomes red or irritated once the strip has dried, do not try this project.

Continued on the next page

3 Continue applying the strips, overlapping them, until you've created the mask shape you want. Don't cover your eyes, nostrils or mouth!

4 Apply two more layers of plaster strips following the same pattern as the first layer.

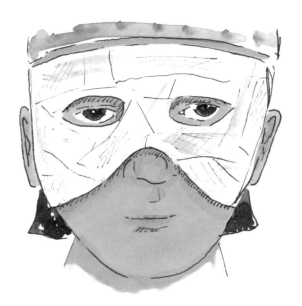

5 In about 10 to 15 minutes, your mask will be firm enough to remove. If you scrunch up your face while holding the mask at the sides, it should come off.

6 Scrunch up a big wad of newspaper and place your mask on it to dry for a day.

7 When your mask is dry, use a hole punch or scissors to make a hole on each side for the elastic, ribbon or string that will hold the mask on.

8 Tie on the elastic, ribbon or string and try your mask on.

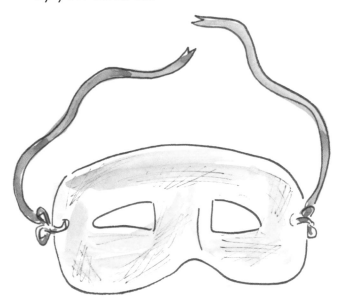

Finishing Features

Once your mask is dry, add special features to your disguise.

1 Tape or glue on fun finds like sponges, paper towels, Plasticine, etc., to create a nose, beak, snout, ears, horns, eyebrows, cheeks, chin, warts, mustache, etc.

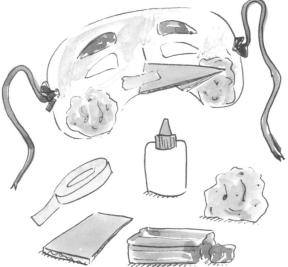

2 Cover the features with two layers of plaster strips. Let dry.

3 Paint your mask with acrylics. Let dry.

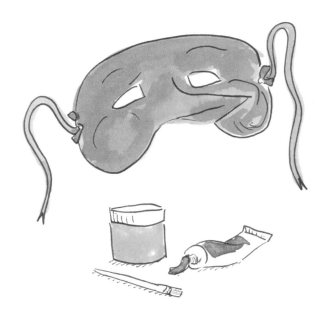

4 Glue on some glitter or other fun finds.

PARTY PIÑATA

Have a bash that's filled with fun and terrific treats by making a piñata — it's a piece of cake!

Artist's Tools

- big balloon
- newspaper
- large plastic bowl
- wallpaper paste
- scissors
- string, ribbon or yarn
- fun finds, cotton batting, pieces of foam, cardboard
- masking tape
- glue
- acrylic paints and brushes
- metallic markers, chalk pastels
- streamers, tissue paper, crepe paper, aluminum foil, glitter, markers, chalk pastels, Model Magic
- candy

1 Blow up a big balloon. Tie a knot in the end.

2 Tear the newspaper into lots of short strips, about 5 cm (2 in.) wide.

3 In a large bowl, mix the wallpaper paste with water, following the instructions on the box.

4 Dip a newspaper strip into the paste mixture. Run the strip through your fingers to remove extra paste. Spread it on the balloon and smooth out any wrinkles with your fingers.

5 Spread papier-mâché strips, one at a time, over the whole balloon. Let dry until the balloon is hard. Then add another layer of papier-mâché. Let dry.

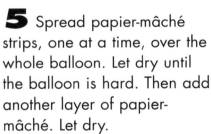

6 Using the scissors, carefully punch a hole in the top of the balloon. It needs to be just big enough to drop in the treats when your piñata is finished. Burst the balloon and remove it.

7 Poke two small holes on each side of the bigger hole. Cut two pieces of string, ribbon or yarn, about 45 cm (18 in.) long. Tie a knot in the ends and thread through the holes.

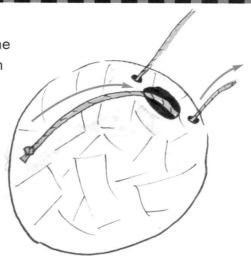

8 Tape and glue on a few fun finds, straws, cotton batting, pieces of foam or a sponge, cardboard or balled-up paper to transform your papier-mâché balloon into a cool creature or silly shape.

9 Cover the balloon and the taped-on features with a layer of papier-mâché. Let dry. Add a third layer, if you like. (Too many layers may make the piñata unbreakable!)

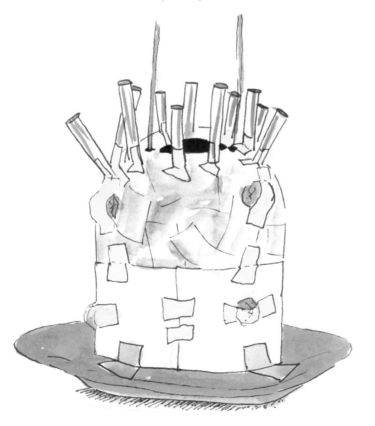

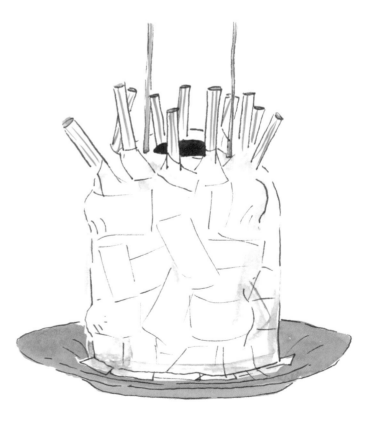

Delicious Decorating Tips

● Paint your piñata with a tasty assortment of acrylic or tempera paints. If you brush on a primer coat of white acrylic paint first, the colors will be brighter.

● Add a pinch of crepe paper, a dash of glitter and a dollop of Model Magic.

Hang It Up

Tie the ends of the string, ribbon or yarn together and hang your piñata from the ceiling.

Animal-shaped piñatas are sure to add to a wonderfully wild party theme!

DYNAMIC DRUMS

Turn your artistic eye into a musical ear! These dynamic drums will inspire some real moving and shaking.

Artist's Tools

- different-sized plant pots (plastic or clay) or other containers, such as recycled juice and coffee cans
- pencils, chopsticks or wooden spoons
- packing tape
- acrylic paints and brushes
- scissors
- fabric pieces
- large elastic bands, string or leather strips
- sponges, rubber balls

1 Line up the pots or cans and turn them upside down — just to test the sounds they make. Perk up your ears and tap the bottoms, one at a time, with a pencil, chopstick or wooden spoon. Hear the difference? The smaller the container, the higher the sound. And the bigger the container, the lower the sound.

2 Turn the pots or cans over. Cover the top of each one with strips of packing tape. The tape should be tight and should completely cover the top.

3 Paint some rhythmic designs on the sides of your drums. What's your favorite musical beat? Wild and crazy? Strong and steady? Clear and classical?

4 Cut out circles of fabric for each drum. Make the circles quite a bit larger than the top of the drums.

5 Spread fabric over the taped top of each drum. Hold the fabric securely in place with elastic bands, string or leather strips.

6 To make drumsticks, stick small sponges on the ends of two pencils or chopsticks. Wrap the sponges in pieces of fabric and tie with string. Or stick small rubber balls on the ends.

WONDERFUL WIND CHIMES

The soft, tinkling sound of these wind chimes will transport you into the loveliest landscapes.

Artist's Tools

- fishing line or strong string
- scissors
- chiming objects: old spoons, forks, keys, small pieces of copper pipe, copper elbows, small metal combs, pieces of fired clay, etc.
- clothes hanger, short dowel or stick, or large metal ring
- modeling clay
- glue

1 Cut four or five different lengths of fishing line or string.

2 Collect your chiming objects and experiment with the different sounds they make by gently bumping them together, a few at a time. Choose four or five objects that have the most interesting sounds, shapes and colors.

3 Tie one end of a length of fishing line or string to each of your objects.

4 Lay the objects flat on a table. Tie them, one by one, to a clothes hanger, dowel, stick or metal ring. Space the objects close enough so that they gently bump each other when shaken.

5 To keep your objects in place, glue modeling clay on the ends of the fishing line or string.

6 Hang your chimes outdoors where the wind can gently blow them:

• on a low tree branch

• from the balcony or porch roof

• in a window

WHISTLING OCARINA

An ocarina is an egg-shaped flute that's made and played by people all around the world. This one is a clay creation that needs to be fired in a kiln. Look for a ceramics shop or potter's studio that offers kiln-drying time and assistance.

Before you start this musical project, check out "Creating with Clay" on pages 104–107.

Artist's Tools

- piece of canvas or plastic
- clay
- fishing line
- pencil or knitting needle
- plastic bag
- access to a kiln

1 Spread canvas or plastic over your worktable to keep your clay from sticking.

2 Cut off a chunk of clay. The best way is to wrap a piece of fishing line around a large piece of clay and pull it through. Store leftover clay in a plastic bag that's tightly closed.

3 You need to wedge the clay to squish out air bubbles (see page 105).

- Throw it onto your canvas.
- Push your palms into it.
- Repeat several times.

4 Roll the clay into an egg-shaped ball. Press your thumb into it and pinch it all the way around until it's hollow in the middle. The walls of the ball should be about 1 cm (½ in.) thick.

5 Leave a small hole in the top. This is where the sound comes from. Blow gently over the top. If there's no sound yet, keep adjusting the hole until you hear a bit of music.

6 Cut off another small piece of clay and roll it into a short, fat snake. Poke a hole through its length with a pencil or knitting needle. This is the mouthpiece.

Continued on the next page

7 To attach the mouthpiece to the body of the ocarina, use a pencil or knitting needle to scratch the surface of each piece where they need to join.

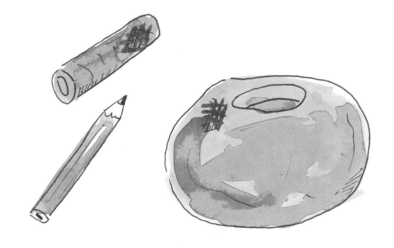

8 Mix some slip (see page 106) and smooth it over the scratched surfaces. Carefully press the two pieces together.

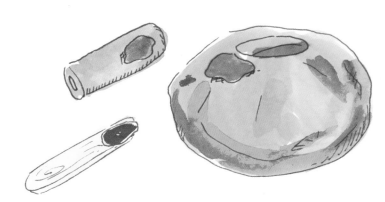

9 Hold it gently and try blowing through the mouthpiece. Are you whistling yet? You can change the sound by adding a few finger holes in the top.

10 Use a pencil or knitting needle to scratch or carve patterns and textures into your ocarina. Or use more slip to attach clay features and turn your ocarina into a musical creature.

11 Place your ocarina in a loose plastic bag and let it dry very slowly. It will take at least a few days.

12 When it's dry, take the ocarina to a ceramics shop or potter's studio to be fired. Ask someone there to help you choose and add a colorful glaze. (Your ocarina will need another firing after being glazed.)

BODY DANCE PUPPET

Make this body dance puppet small enough for one or big enough for a whole crew. Then get up and dance!

Artist's Tools

- cardboard box (large enough to cover your head and shoulders)
- scissors or utility knife
- acrylic paints and brushes
- metallic markers
- old sheet, curtain, bedspread or large piece of fabric
- fabric paint, glue, glitter
- beads, buttons, bows and other fun finds
- twine or strong string

Creating a Head

1 With an adult's help, cut off the flaps of the box. Cut out some spectacular eyes, some ornate ears, an expressive mouth. For a more elaborate mouth, glue or tape on a smaller box.

2 Use acrylic paints and a fat brush to paint big, bold designs.

3 Use a smaller brush and metallic markers to add delicate details.

Making a Body

4 Try on the sheet, curtain, bedspread or fabric. It needs to be long enough to cover you — or all of your crew — and wide enough to cover your outstretched arms.

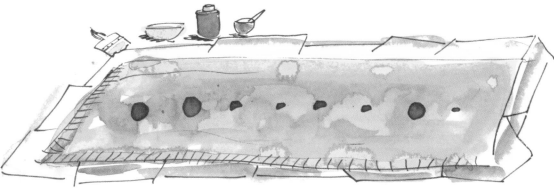

5 Lay the fabric flat. Brush on some dancing designs with the fabric paint and glue and glitter. Let dry. Cut some fringes along the edges of the body and add some fun finds.

6 Poke two holes in the back of the headpiece. Thread the twine or string through and tie the fabric to the headpiece.

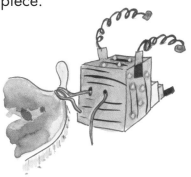

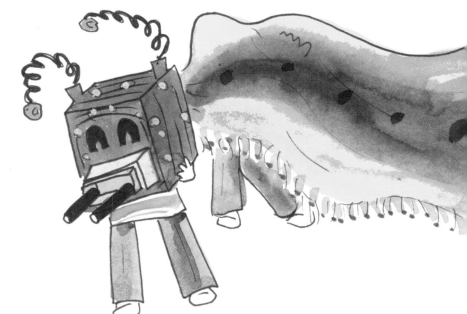

WILD-THING PUPPETS

Let your imagination run wild with this plaster puppet project.

Artist's Tools

- newspaper
- cardboard tubes
- masking tape
- glue gun
- Plasticine or Model Magic
- big garbage bag
- roll of plaster tape
- bowl or container
- large piece of fabric
- markers
- scissors
- needle and thread or fabric glue
- ribbon or string
- acrylic paints and brushes
- fun finds

Create a Hideous Head

1 Scrunch up some newspapers into a head shape. Tape the head (or heads) to a cardboard tube or toilet paper roll.

2 Make hooked horns, evil eyes, a nasty nose and terrible teeth with Plasticine or Model Magic. With an adult's help, attach the creature's features to the head with a glue gun.

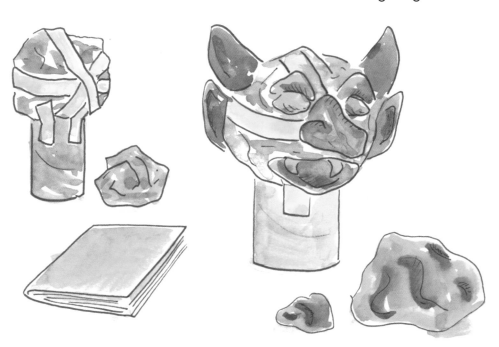

3 Cover your work surface with a garbage bag. Cut short strips of plaster tape. Dip the strips, one at a time, in a bowl of water and completely cover the puppet head and tube. Add one or two more layers. Allow each layer to dry.

Make a Fabric Body

4 Fold the fabric in half, with the right side on the inside, and lay it on your worktable.

5 Place your hand on top of the fabric, keeping your middle three fingers together and extending your thumb and little finger. With a marker, trace an outline that's 2.5 cm (1 in.) larger than your hand all the way around. Cut out the body.

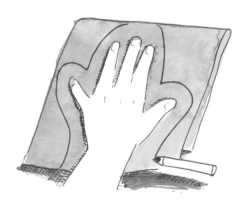

6 Put the fabric together, wrong sides out. Sew or glue the side seams about 1 cm (½ in.) from the edge. Leave a hole at the top for the head and at the bottom for your hand.

7 Turn the body right side out and insert the puppet head in the top. Tie a ribbon or string tightly around the neck tube and fabric.

Paint and Decorate

With acrylics, paint the puppet's face. Glue on buttons, googly eyes, beads and other fun finds.

PUPPET THEATER

Search your imagination high and low, and create the perfect place to stage your next wild-thing puppet performance.

Artist's Tools

- large cardboard box
- utility knife or scissors
- ruler
- plastic sheet
- acrylic paints
- sponges and paintbrushes
- containers for water and mixing paints
- two wooden sticks or dowels, if needed
- masking tape

Make a Stage

1 Ask an adult to help you cut off the top, bottom and one long side of the cardboard box.

2 Use a pencil and a ruler to mark a large window in the center panel of your cardboard. Ask for help cutting the window out.

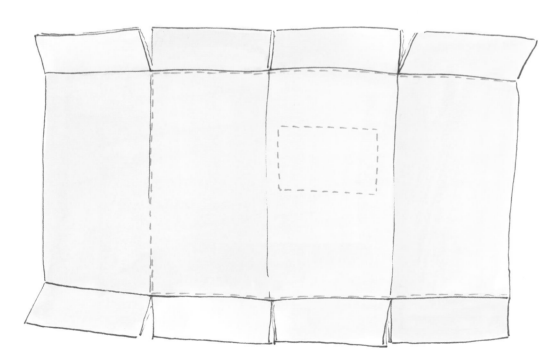

Paint Some Scenes

3 Cover the floor with a plastic sheet. Lay the stage flat on the floor.

4 Prime the surface of the stage for painting (see page 68). Let dry.

5 For the background (the images that are farthest away), use a sponge and watered-down paint. Let dry.

6 For the middle ground (images that are in the middle distance), mix a little white with the colors and use a medium-sized brush. Let dry.

7 For the foreground (images that are closest), apply pure color with a small brush. Let dry.

8 Stand your puppet theater up. If it's a little wobbly, make a hole in each corner and insert the ends of a wooden stick or dowel into the holes so that one stick goes across the top and one goes across the bottom. Use masking tape to hold the sticks in place.

SHADOW PUPPETS

Have you got a story idea lurking in your imagination? Create some shadow-puppet characters and put on a play.

Artist's Tools

- pencil and sketchbook
- bristol board
- scissors and hole punch
- brass fasteners
- bamboo sticks
- masking tape
- white sheet
- lamp
- small table

Puppet Parts

1 Make a few quick sketches of your characters.

2 On the bristol board, draw the separate body parts of your puppets: upper legs, lower legs, upper arms, forearms, hands, feet, torso, neck and head.

3 Cut out the puppet parts. Use the hole punch to add some features.

4 Attach the puppet parts by punching holes in the joints or "pivot points" and attaching the parts with brass fasteners.

5 Tape a bamboo stick to each of the puppet's body parts that you want to move.

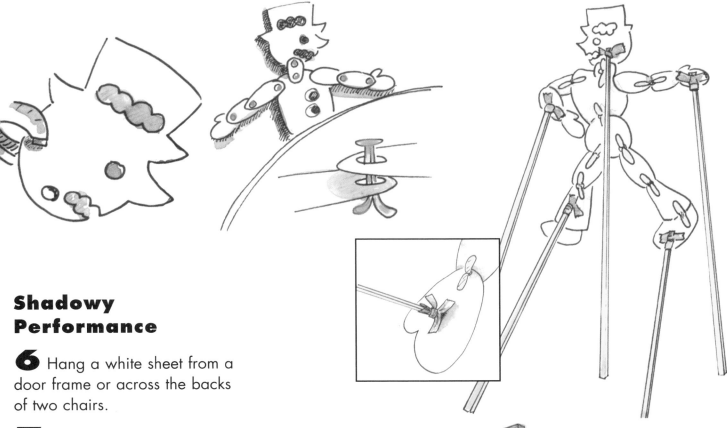

Shadowy Performance

6 Hang a white sheet from a door frame or across the backs of two chairs.

7 Place a lamp on a small table behind the sheet. Leave enough room between the lamp and the sheet for you and your puppets to move freely.

8 Darken the room. Turn on the lamp. Let the play begin!

MYTHICAL SCROLL

What's your favorite mythical creature or symbol? A fire-breathing dragon? A snow-white unicorn? Use some mythical ideas to create a scroll full of images and symbols that mean something special to you.

Artist's Tools

- pencil and sketchbook
- rubber gloves and plastic sheet
- paper fabric or light white cotton, about 60 cm by 1.2 m (2 ft. by 4 ft.)
- metallic pens and markers
- favorite colors of food coloring
- plastic containers for mixing colors
- paintbrushes
- dowels or bamboo sticks, about 60 cm (2 ft.) long
- white glue or tacks
- Plasticine or Model Magic

1 Sketch some simple drawings of mythical creatures and special symbols.

2 Cover your worktable with the plastic sheet and put on your rubber gloves. Lay the paper fabric or cotton flat on the table.

3 Use metallic pens and permanent markers to draw or trace your images and symbols on your scroll.

4 Pour a bit of each color of food coloring into a plastic container.

5 Around your symbols, brush on a background of colors that have mythical or symbolic meaning for you (for some ideas, see below). Let dry.

6 Glue or tack the short ends of your scroll to the sticks. Press some Plasticine knobs on the stick ends. Now you can roll up your scroll or hang it on your door.

Symbolic Colors   Here is what some colors symbolize:

Blue	**Green**	**Orange**	**Purple**	**Red**	**Yellow**
truth	life	happiness	royalty	love	beauty
loyalty	youth	luxury	pride	strength	goodness
peace	hope	fire	justice	bravery	intelligence

FLYING SEA SERPENT

Many myths and legends feature winged sea serpents that look a lot like dragons. This sea serpent is large enough to fly away with you!

Build the body

Artist's Tools

- work gloves
- chicken wire
- wire cutters
- body-sized cardboard box
- twist-ties
- roll of paper fabric
- spray bottle, water
- white glue
- large bowl
- fat paint brush

1 Ask an adult to help cut the chicken wire so that it's long enough to wrap around the cardboard box with some overlap.

2 Wearing work gloves, wrap the chicken wire loosely around the box. Use twist-ties to tie the wire together at the side, front and rear.

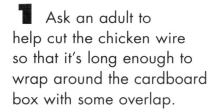

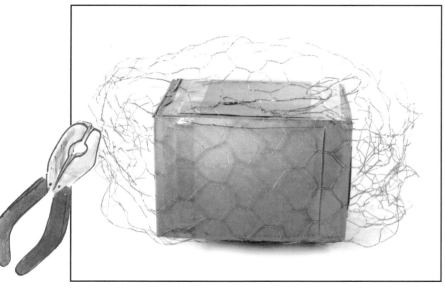

3 Cut one or two pieces of fabric long enough to wrap around the serpent's body.

4 On a covered surface, spray the fabric with water until wet. Wrap the wet fabric around the body, leaving a small section of chicken wire uncovered at both ends.

5 Pour some white glue into a large container. Use a fat brush to apply a coat of glue to the wet body. Let dry.

Make the Tail

Artist's Tools

- old pantyhose, pants or shirt
- foam chips or newspapers
- twine or strong string

6 Stuff the pantyhose legs with foam chips or newspapers. Or cut off one leg of an old pair of pants or the sleeve of an old shirt, and stuff. For a really long tail, sew or tie two or three pairs of pantyhose legs, two pant legs or two sleeves together after stuffing.

7 Tie the tail to the chicken wire at one end of the body.

8 If you want to paint the tail later, cover it with paper fabric and the glue mixture. Let dry.

Continued on the next page

Construct the Head

Artist's Tools

- head-sized cardboard box
- egg cartons
- white glue or a glue gun
- cardboard, Plasticine or Model Magic
- scissors
- string or twine

9 To make the serpent's mouth, glue the egg cartons to the cardboard box. If you're using a glue gun, ask an adult to help.

10 Create other serpent features by cutting them out of cardboard or molding them out of Plasticine or Model Magic. Glue them on.

11 Punch a few holes in the back of the head, and tie the head to the chicken-wire body.

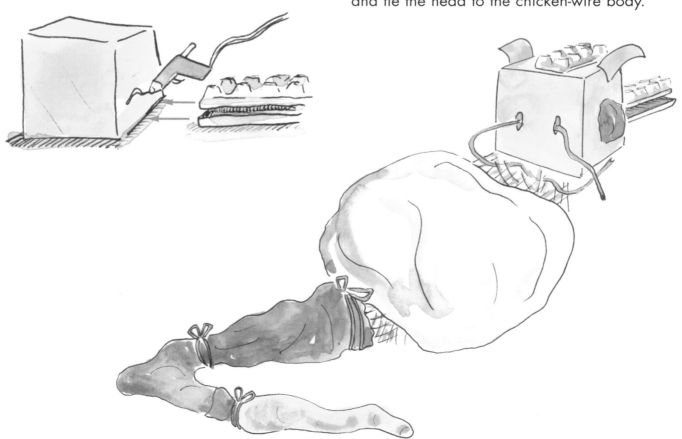

Create the Wings

Artist's Tools

- scissors
- two wing-sized, wing-shaped branches
- twine, string or duct tape
- aluminum foil
- colored tissue paper
- spray bottle, water and white glue

12 With an adult's help, use scissors to cut a hole in both sides of the body. Insert one end of a branch in each hole. Use twine, string or duct tape to hold them in place.

13 Cut out large pieces of aluminum foil and tissue paper. Cover the wings with a layer of aluminum foil and then a layer of colored tissue paper.

14 In a spray bottle, mix equal parts of white glue and water and shake well. Spray the tissue with the mixture until wet. Let dry.

Paint and Decorate

- Brush on acrylic paints.
- Glue on glitter.
- Attach fun finds.

I think I'll call him Fluffy

TREASURE BOX

A treasure box should be as special as the treasure it contains. Create a treasure box that reflects the brilliance buried in you.

Artist's Tools

- cardboard boxes, various sizes
- strong glue, masking tape
- scissors
- wrapping paper, wallpaper, aluminum foil, old comics, magazine pictures, artwork, etc.
- Model Magic, clay, Plasticine
- fun finds (buttons, yarn, bottle caps, toys, sticks, stones, cardboard tubes, old pencils, paintbrushes, etc.)
- markers, acrylic paints and brushes

Treasure Hunt

Boxes come in all shapes and sizes. Look around for one that's just right for the treasure you plan to put inside.

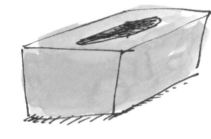

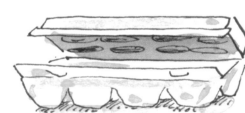

Wrap It Up

Capture the character of your treasures by wrapping your box or cardboard tubes in wacky wallpaper, shiny aluminum foil, comic covers or your own artwork.

Top It Up

Make a treasured scene on top using all your favorite fun finds. A towering turret? Giant gems? Racing cars? Glue on some creative handles made from old toys, cardboard, clay or Model Magic.

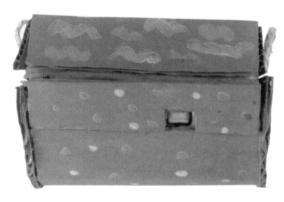

Decorate It

Add highlights with acrylic paints, and glue on some delightful decorations.

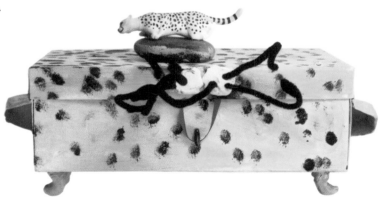

HAUNTING DIORAMA

Here's a haunting idea. Create a spooky 3-D scene in a box — called a diorama — and scare yourself silly!

Artist's Tools

- rectangular cardboard box with a lid, such as a shoebox
- scissors
- piece of red cellophane
- glue
- acrylic or tempera paints and brushes
- chalk pastels
- construction paper, aluminum foil, tissues, fabric, cotton balls, pipe cleaners, toothpicks, fun finds, etc.
- Plasticine or Model Magic
- thread, string or yarn
- shish-kebab sticks or Popsicle sticks
- tape

1 Cut a large window out of the front of the box. Cut a smaller window out of one side. Glue the red cellophane over the smaller window.

2 Cut a few narrow slots in the other side and top of the box.

3 Paint the inside of the box and lid with a combination of creepy colors.

4 With the chalk pastels, draw some scary shadows and scenes on the painted sides of the box.

5 Create some horrible creatures and freaky furniture.

- Use Plasticine or Model Magic to make spiders, witches, bats and goblins. Use thread, string or yarn to make spider webs.

- Use cardboard, Plasticine and fun finds to make creaky stairs, trapdoors, eerie artwork, tables, coffins, etc.

6 Attach the creatures and furniture to the box with glue, tape or toothpicks stuck into bits of Plasticine.

7 Attach some creepy creatures to sticks and poke the ends through the slots so you can move them.

SILLY CIRCUS

Here's a circus you don't have to run away to join! Create your own clowns, wild animals, amazing acrobats and death-defying stunts.

Clowns, Wild Animals, Trick Riders

Artist's Tools

- pipe cleaners, wire
- Plasticine or Model Magic
- glue
- buttons, beads, marshmallows
- markers
- fun finds (fabric pieces, paper clips, faux fur, etc.)

1 Make some pipe-cleaner clowns and wild, wiry animals.

2 Fatten them up with Plasticine or Model Magic, marshmallows, buttons and beads.

3 Decorate with fun finds.

4 Create unicycles and stilts from wire or pipe cleaners, and take some of your circus clowns and animals for a ride.

Amazing Acrobats

Artist's Tools

- wire or pipe cleaners
- small block of wood
- cardboard
- strong white glue
- elastic band
- hairnet

1 Create a few wiry acrobats.

2 Glue a small block of wood to a piece of cardboard. Let dry.

3 Loop the elastic band around the wood block. Pull the elastic band back.

4 Get your acrobats ready and release!

5 See if you can land your acrobats safely in a nearby net.

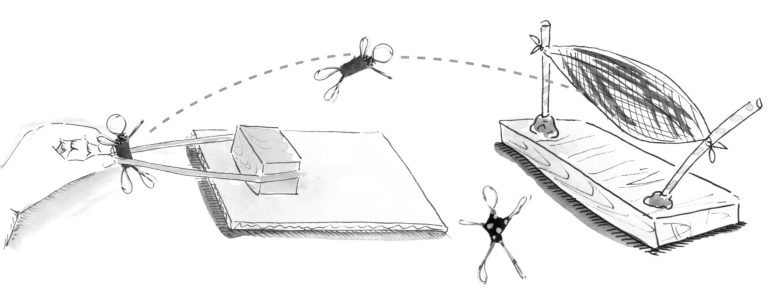

Incredible Air Show

3 Tape the wings to the straw.

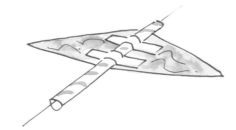

- fishing line
- plastic straw
- masking tape
- construction paper
- metallic markers
- balloon

1 Thread the fishing line through the straw. Tape each end of the line to something secure, such as the back of a chair and a doorframe.

4 Blow up the balloon. Tape it to the bottom of your straw — and let go.

2 Cut two paper wings from a piece of construction paper. Use metallic markers to create some streamlined designs.

Death Drop

Artist's Tools

- pencil
- spool of string
- cardboard
- scissors
- pipe cleaner
- straw
- button or bead
- paper cup
- tape or string

1 Run the pencil through the spool of string.

2 Cut a piece of cardboard 13 cm (about 5 in.) wide and twice as long as the pencil. Fold the cardboard into a C-shape.

3 Poke the pencil through both ends.

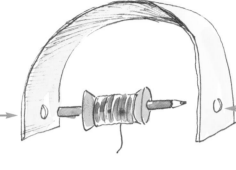

4 Make a handle for your pencil with a pipe cleaner, a straw and a big button or bead. Attach the handle to the pencil.

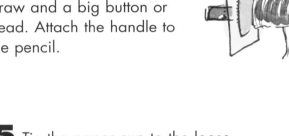

5 Tie the paper cup to the loose end of the string. Tape or tie the cardboard piece to the back of a chair or a banister. Bombs away!

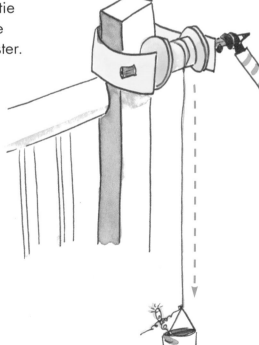

RECYCLED ROBOT

Use your artistic eye to transform a pile of recycled materials into a remarkable robot. If you'd like your robot to blink and move, wire it up with a few electrical supplies from a hardware store. An adult will have great fun helping with this project.

Artist's Tools

- recycled materials: cardboard boxes, cardboard tubes, egg cartons, corks, Popsicle sticks, tin cans, plastic bottles, aluminum foil, wire, string, old knobs, plastic gloves, old clothes, broken toys, etc.
- glue gun
- duct tape
- scissors
- latex or acrylic paints and brushes
- metallic markers
- Plasticine or Model Magic
- fun finds

Construct a Robot Body

Let your pile of junk inspire some ideas. Do your recycled materials add up to a robot that's a humanoid, a dog-oid or a chicken-oid?

1 Transform your big pieces of recycled junk into a robot body. Ask an adult to help attach the parts with a glue gun and duct tape.

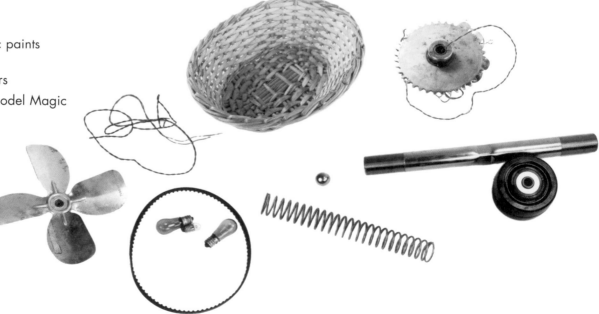

2 Paint the body with latex or acrylic paints. Add highlights with metallic markers. Or glue on some foil.

3 Mold robotic features with Plasticine or Model Magic and glue on.

4 Add some character with fun finds.

Continued on the next page

Light Up Your Robot

Ask an adult to help create a current that will make your robot light up.

Electrical Supplies

- scissors or wire cutters
- 14 or 24 gauge electrical wire
- 1.5 or 2.5 volt lightbulbs
- 1.5 volt C or D cell batteries
- electrical tape
- wooden clothespin

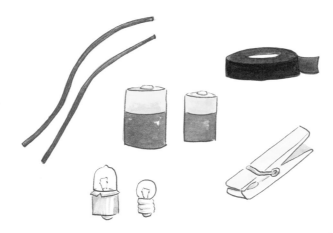

1 Carefully strip about 5 cm (2 in.) of the plastic coating off the ends of two pieces of wire with a pair of scissors or wire cutters.

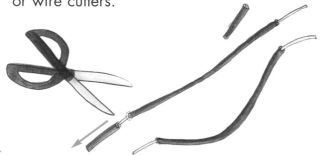

2 Wrap an end of one wire around the base of your lightbulb. Tape it to the positive end of your battery (the side marked with a plus sign).

3 Use another small piece of tape to attach an end of the second wire to the negative side of your battery (the side marked with a minus sign).

4 Wrap the free end of each wire to the ends of a wooden clothespin (the part that you squeeze together).

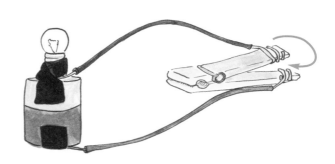

5 Press the ends of your clothespin together to complete the current and light up the bulb.

6 Look for parts of your recycled r(
light up! Duct tape, electrical tape, mode⌐..
clay, string or wires are all helpful for
attaching or inserting a current.

WACKY CLOCK

Take a wacky idea and turn it into a timely sculpture. What form will your clock take? A hamburger? A masked bandit? The Queen of Hearts?

Artist's Tools

- pencil and sketchbook
- working parts of a clock and a battery (available at craft stores)
- ruler
- sheet of foam core, cardboard or bristol board
- scissors or utility knife
- cardboard box with a tight-fitting lid
- white glue
- metallic markers or pens
- old magazines
- acrylic or tempera paints and brushes
- Model Magic, pipe cleaners, wrapping paper, magazine pictures, fun finds, etc.

1 Draw a few wacky clock ideas in your sketchbook. Choose your favorite one.

2 Measure the size of the clock parts so you know how big to make your clock face.

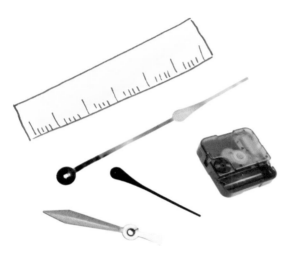

3 Draw a simple clock face shape on your sheet of foam core or cardboard. Make sure your shape is larger than the clock parts.

4 Cut out the clock face. Ask an adult to help if you're using a utility knife.

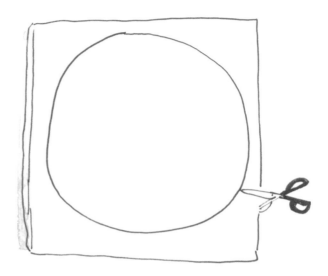

5 Poke a hole in the center of the clock face. Press the "nub" or screw attached to the clock motor through the hole.

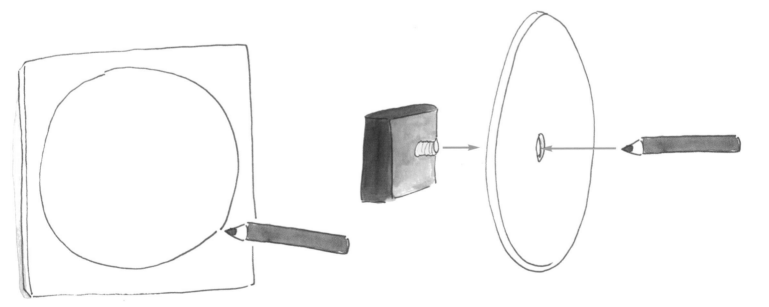

Continued on the next page

6 Attach the hands — they should slide or screw onto the "nub" or screw poking through the clock face.

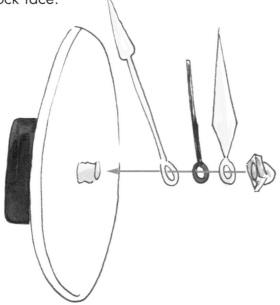

7 Cut a hole in the cardboard box lid that's just large enough to fit snugly around the clock motor.

8 Place a bit of glue on the back of the clock face and attach it to the box lid. Put the lid on the box.

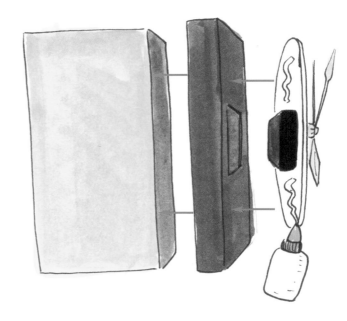

9 Draw the hours on your clock face with metallic or permanent markers. Or cut out numbers and glue them on.

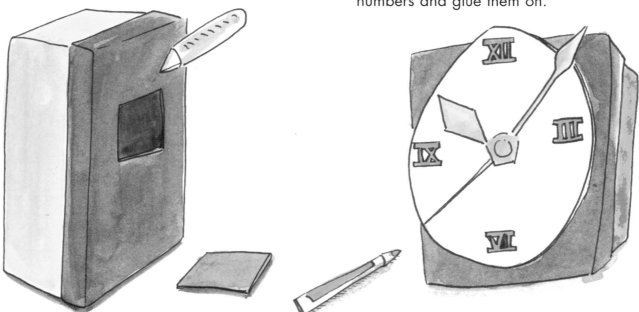

10 Decorate your clock.

• Use markers and magazine cutouts to make a funny face.

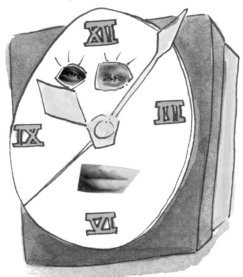

• Glue on arms, legs and funny features made from Model Magic, feathers, beads, pipe cleaners and fun finds.

• Paint on crazy colors with acrylic paints.

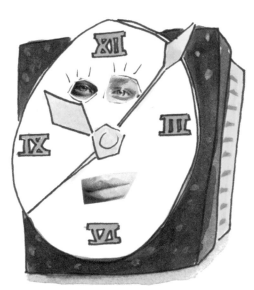

11 To get your clock ticking, insert the battery.

FAIRY HEADBOARD

Design a fantastic headboard for your bed so the fairies can watch over you while you sleep.

- large, square cardboard box
- scissors or utility knife
- tape measure
- hole punch
- pencil and sketchbook
- acrylic or latex paints and brushes
- metallic pens, markers
- Model Magic, pipe cleaners, stencils, etc.
- ribbon or twine

1 Ask an adult to help cut along one fold of your box. Lay the cardboard flat on the floor.

2 Cut off the flaps and along the center fold so your cardboard is in two halves. You will only need one half to make your headboard.

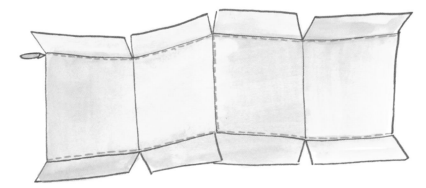

3 Fold your cardboard piece in half and place it over your bed's headboard to make sure it fits. If it's too big, you may have to measure the length and width of your headboard and cut the cardboard to fit.

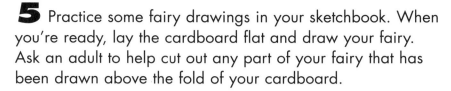

4 Punch a small hole halfway down each side of the folded cardboard, about 2.5 cm (1 in.) from the edge.

5 Practice some fairy drawings in your sketchbook. When you're ready, lay the cardboard flat and draw your fairy. Ask an adult to help cut out any part of your fairy that has been drawn above the fold of your cardboard.

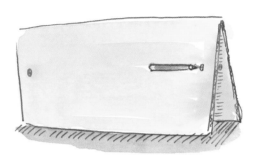

6 Paint and decorate your headboard.

- Brush on a background scene with acrylic or latex paint.

- Create some details with metallic pens, markers or paints.

- Print some stenciled borders (see page 73 for making stencils).

- Mold some fun shapes out of Model Magic and attach them with pipe cleaners.

7 Slip your finished fairy headboard over your old headboard and keep it in place by threading ribbon or twine through the holes and tying it together.

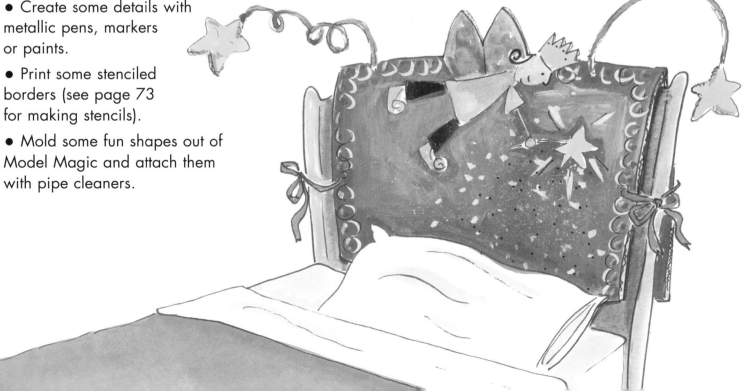

PERFECT PRIVACY

Everyone needs some private space to create in. Or just to hide in. Turn a super-sized cardboard box into a really neat room divider.

Artist's Tools

- pencil and paper
- tape measure or measuring stick
- huge cardboard box (such as a refrigerator box)
- scissors or utility knife
- white latex paint (primer)
- acrylic paints, paintbrushes, sponges, stencils, markers, fun finds

Design

Sometimes making a design or plan before you cut, glue and paint can save you lots of artistic time and trouble.

- Sketch some ideas. How about a turret-style top? Some holes to peek out from?

- Measure your room. How big can your big-box divider be?

- Turn your ideas and measurements into a design or plan.

Build

1 Cut off the flaps of the big box. Cut along one of the folds to open it up. If you're using a utility knife, ask an adult to help.

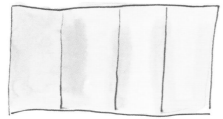

2 Lay the cardboard flat. Brush a primer coat of white latex paint on the front. Put some weights (bricks, old telephone books, etc.) along the edges so the divider doesn't buckle as it dries. When the front is dry, prime the back. Let dry.

3 Draw your design onto the front and back. If your design has cut-outs, use a utility knife.

Decorate

• Use acrylics to paint your private place.

• Glue on cardboard cut-outs to add an extra dimension.

• Use stencils if your design includes repeated patterns (see page 73).

• Attach some fun finds.

FANTASTIC FRAMES

Create fantastic frames for your favorite works of art. Then hang them up for all the world to see.

1 Find a flat surface that's slightly larger than your artwork, such as a piece of bristol board, a paper plate or a piece of wood.

2 Spread glue around the edges of your pictures and press them on the frames. The artwork doesn't have to be perfectly centered in the frames. Placing pictures slightly off center adds a little excitement.

3 Decorate with

- paints
- markers
- scissors
- glitter glue, tape, tacks and fun finds

PARADE OF PEDESTALS

Create and paint some perfect pedestals to show off your sculptural masterpieces.

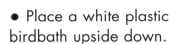

- Place a white plastic birdbath upside down.
- Pile and paint some cardboard boxes.

- Stack two large clay flowerpots with open ends together. Paint with acrylics.

- Set a wooden crate on its side and cover with plain fabric.

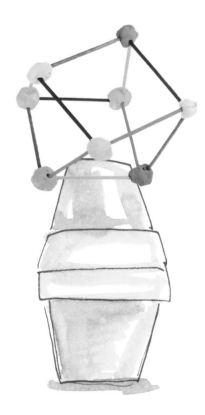

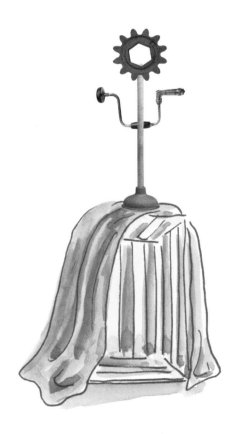

INSPIRATIONAL INSTALLATIONAL

Use all your creative confidence to display your amazing art. It's an installation that's sure to inspire!

- Hang up an amazing mural.

- Place a super sculpture in a special spot.

- Unroll your favorite crazy carpet.

- Display a dynamic diorama.

- Frame a few interesting images.

Inspirational Ideas

By giving your art projects a particular theme, you can create the most amazing installations. Themes to think about

- a reflecting garden
- a room of rainbows
- a prehistoric home
- a medieval castle
- a winter wonderland
- an underwater world

The Avenue Road Arts School Artists

The Avenue Road Arts School was founded in Toronto, Canada, in 1993. It's a place where everyone can become an artistic adventurer and where making art — all kinds of art — is a great way to discover your many hidden talents and a soaring imagination.

As your guides, we want every artistic adventurer to be excited about taking those steps toward artistic discovery. That's why the activities in this book reflect both the experience and know-how of the artists who have gone before us and a playful attitude that we think makes learning fun.

After traveling through these pages with us, we hope that you have found your creative confidence and discovered that you really can draw, paint, sculpt and build a wonderful world.

Who We Are at Avenue Road

Liana Del Mastro Vicente: Painting, Sculpture, Mixed Media

Julie Frost: Sculpture, Mixed Media

Leslie Graham: Drawing, Painting, Printmaking, Mixed Media

Martha Johnson: Painting, Sculpture

Irene Luxbacher: Drawing, Painting, Sculpture, Mixed Media

Joni Moriyama: Ceramic Sculpture, Mixed Media

Eric Neighbour: Ceramic Sculpture, Mixed Media

Linda Prussick: Drawing, Painting, Sculpture, Mixed Media

Cynthia Sneath: Mixed Media

Susie Whaley: Mixed Media

Russell Zeid: Kinetic Sculpture

GLOSSARY

Architecture
The design and making of buildings.

Armature
A framework or skeleton that supports a clay sculpture.

Art
Creative thought expressed as drawing, painting, sculpture, music, movement or writing.

Assemblage
A sculpture made of a variety of materials, such as scraps of wood, cloth, string, cardboard and metal.

Balance
Parts of art, such as its lines, shapes and forms, arranged to have equal weight.

Carving
Cutting a figure or design into wood, stone or other hard materials.

Color
See hue.

Color wheel
A circle made up of the primary colors (red, yellow and blue) and the secondary colors (green, orange and violet). Complementary colors are opposite each other on the wheel, and analogous colors are beside each other.

Contour drawing
To draw only the outline of a body or an object.

Cross-hatching
To use criss-crossing lines to add shadows or value to a drawing.

Depth
A way of describing the feeling of space in three-dimensional art.

Dimension
The measurement of an object's height, width or depth. Flat objects have two dimensions (height and width) and objects with volume have three dimensions (height, width and depth).

Drawing
See contour drawing; figure drawing; gesture drawing

Figure drawing
To draw a person's body.

Foreshortening
An artist's technique for creating a feeling of depth on a flat surface. Foreshortened figures often look as though they will pop right off the page.

Form
The shape of an object that has many sides or viewpoints.

Found objects
Everyday objects in your environment, such as a tin can, stick, toy or feather.

Gesture drawing
To draw using quick lines, shapes and scribbles.

Graffiti
Drawing, painting or writing on a wall, door or public place.

Harmony
A pleasing combination of lines, shapes, colors or forms.

Highlight
A brightly lit spot on an object or image.

Hue
Another word for color. Red, yellow, blue, green, orange and violet are all different hues.

Impasto
Paint thickly applied with a brush, palette knife or hand.

Installation
Art made to be part of the space or room that it's in.

Kinetic Art
Art made of moveable parts.

Landscape
A scene or view of the outdoors.

Line
A continuous straight or curved mark. Lines can be two-dimensional (such as one made with a pencil mark on paper) or three-dimensional (such as one made with a piece of wire).

Medium
The material used to make a piece of art.

Mixed Media
Art made using a combination of tools, materials and techniques.

Modeling
Shaping or forming material into art.

Negative Space
The empty area around an image or sculpture.

Perspective
The way artists create the feeling of three-dimensions or depth on a flat surface.

Positive Space
The area an image or sculpture fills up.

Proportion
How the size, shape or amount of one thing compares to another.

Scale
The size of an object or image.

Sculpture
Three-dimensional art, such as a papier-mâché figure or a mobile.

Scumbling
A technique in which almost dry paint is brushed over dry paint so that the second color still shows through.

Sgraffito
A technique in which a layer of paint is scraped off to reveal another color of paint beneath.

Shade
The dark or shadowed part of a picture or photograph. Shade also describes a color that has been mixed with black.

Shading
The dark lines, marks or smudges used to fill in a sketch or drawing.

Shape
A definite or particular form that an object or image has. Rectangles, squares, cylinders, triangles, etc., are all common shapes.

Space
See negative space; positive space

Stencil
A sheet of cardboard, paper or plastic that has a design or lettering cut out of it. When paint or ink is brushed over top of a stencil, the design or lettering will be left on the surface underneath.

Still Life
Stationary or unmoving objects arranged to be drawn, painted or reconstructed by an artist.

Stipple
To draw or paint using dots, flecks or speckles in order to add shadows or color.

Texture
How rough or smooth something feels or looks like it feels.

Tint
A color that has been mixed with white.

Tone
A color that has been mixed with gray.

Value
How light or dark a piece of art is.

Wedging
Pushing, kneeding or squeezing air bubbles out of a chunk of clay.

INDEX